This is the story of how a boy from a poor background benefited from the new opportunities available in the post-1945 era to attend a very good grammar school, gain entry to Oxford University and eventually became a professor at a top grade university, King's College, London.

Early chapters show how hard it was to get a foothold on the lowest rungs of the academic ladder, particularly in a subject, military history, where there were virtually no established positions. No matter how talented and industrious, good fortune played a crucial role, as in so many careers, in helping Brian Bond at a critical stage. By a remarkable coincidence, since Brian was reading some of his books at Oxford, Basil (later Sir Basil) Liddell Hart came to live in the village and promptly gave him tremendous encouragements and support. Liddell Hart, at that time probably the best known military writer in the world, provided wonderful references which, after numerous setbacks, led to junior academic appointment at Exeter and Liverpool universities. Equally important Liddell Hart introduced Brian to Michael Howard (now Sir Michael Howard OM) who was just beginning to pioneer the study of military history-war studies at King's College, London. Michael had a difficult time in persuading the academic establishment that this was a respectable and very important new field of study, but in 1965 he succeeded in setting up a Department of War Studies, and in the following year recruited Brian as a Lecturer in Military History. Promotion was necessarily slow in a tiny department, but Brian was eventually elevated to Reader and then Professor.

The central chapters in this personal memoir provide a frank account of what it was like to teach military history at all levels (but especially to MA and PhD candidates) in the late 20th century. From the outset the students were drawn from virtually every country in the free world and competition for entry was tough. Numbers of staff and students increased steadily through the 1970s and 1980s, but then there was a sudden dramatic expansion as the Department admitted undergraduates for the first time. The range of subjects taught also widened impressively with more emphasis placed on contemporary Strategic Studies. But the 'philosophy' inculcated by Michael Howard; namely the disinterested study of warfare in a broad social and political context continued to provide the Department's teaching.

On the personal level Brian Bond contrasts successes and achievements with 'bad days' in the office and the lecture hall which will strike a chord with all fellow teachers. He also pens a lively account of some of his overseas travels, particularly in Canada, the United States, Pakistan and Japan as well as attending numerous conferences in Europe. In the penultimate chapter 'Books do Furnish a Room' he describes how and why his own books came to be written, and how they were received.

The extra theme or dimension which raises this account above the personal is the remarkable development of military history during Brian Bond's career. Even in the late 1950s scarcely any military history courses were offered in British universities, and there was not a single department. By 2000 the picture had changed drastically with several centres of excellence in the field and with strong interest and support from students. Since then there have been further positive developments which have been surveyed in a concluding chapter entitled 'The Legacy'. Since Brian retired in 2001 he has had only a marginal connection with these later trends but has been given invaluable help in this survey from several colleagues, especially Sir Hew Strachan and Professor Martin Alexander.

It is not for the author to assess his own contribution to the development of military history-war studies, nor to claim that the Department at King's College was the sole pioneer of the new academic subject. But Brian can accurately, if immodestly, point out that he spent thirty five years in the Department (and participating in the wider ramifications of the subject), contributed a substantial variety of books and other publications and, perhaps most importantly, supervised fifty successful PhD candidates, several of whom are now outstanding leaders in the field.

About the author

Brian Bond spent most of his teaching career at King's College London where he played a role in developing the Department of Wars Studies from its very early days in the 1960s. He was awarded a personal chair in Military History and was also appointed a Fellow of the College (FKC). He was President of the Commission for Military History (BCMH) from 1986 to 2006, and was a Visiting Fellow at Brasenose College and, later, at All Souls College, Oxford. He delivered the Lees Knowles Lectures at Cambridge in 2000, published two years later as *The Unquiet Western Front*. His other numerous publications range, in time, from *Victorian Army and the Staff College* (1972) to *Britain's Two World Wars against Germany* (2014). Other noteworthy books include *British Military Policy between the Two World Wars* (1980) and *Survivors of a Kind. Memoirs of the Western Front* (2008). He has been extremely fortunate to be able to combine an academic career in London while living most of his life, with his wife Madeleine, in a beautiful village in the Thames Valley.

Military Historian

My Part in the Birth and Development of War Studies 1966–2016

Brian Bond

Helion & Company Limited

Helion & Company Limited
26 Willow Road
Solihull
West Midlands
B91 1UE
England
Tel. 0121 705 3393
Fax 0121 711 4075
Email: info@helion.co.uk
Website: www.helion.co.uk
Twitter: @helionbooks
Visit our blog http://blog.helion.co.uk/

Published by Helion & Company 2018
Designed and typeset by Mach 3 Solutions Ltd (www.mach3solutions.co.uk)
Cover designed by Paul Hewitt, Battlefield Design (www.battlefield-design.co.uk)
Printed by Short Run Press, Exeter, Devon

ISBN 978-1-912390-40-3

British Library Cataloguing-in-Publication Data.
A catalogue record for this book is available from the British Library.

Contents

List of Photographs

Acknowledgements

I am grateful to John Bourne for reading my typescript at an early stage and saving me from making several errors.

Peter Simkins provided me with a photograph of himself, and Sir Michael Howard permitted me to reprint his photograph as Regius Professor at Oxford from his memoirs *Captain Professor*.

Information about the department of war studies since my retirement was provided by Jayne Peake and Brian Holden Reid for King's College, London; and Gary Sheffield for Wolverhampton University. Sir Hew Strachan gave me such a detailed report on the current state of military history and war studies at Oxford and in Scotland that I have incorporated most of it in my text. Martin Alexander's nuanced, reflective essay on the advances and setbacks of this academic field in British universities generally is published here in full as an appendix.

Once again Emily McLeish deserves my special thanks for so promptly and accurately typing my longhand draft and for sending numerous emails; while my neighbour (and her mother) Penny provided very efficient liaison between us.

Duncan Rogers has been a sympathetic publisher and a good friend during what has been a difficult year for both of us.

My wife Madeleine has not contributed directly to this book, but without her support and encouragement it could not have been written.

Medmenham, Bucks
February 2018

Preface

Old men forget, but they also look back and reflect on how the promising, energetic youth and young man has morphed into the tired and dispirited octogenarian.

In my own case I seek to trace how the sport-obsessed youth became a professor at a first-rank university. This could easily result in a complacent ego-trip, but I feel sufficiently distanced and detached to treat this distant young man fairly objectively, giving due emphasis to the part played by good fortune assisted by vital inspiration and encouragement by teachers and mentors at critical times.

A reviewer might say that I am simply a typical beneficiary of the post-1945 opening up of grammar schools to poor but able boys (and girls) who could not have afforded the time or money to enjoy the opportunity before. This of course is true, but it is not the whole truth as I shall try to show. For the moment it is enough to say that I started well down in the pack. Both of my parents had left village schools as soon as the law allowed (i.e. at 14) and no members of either of their families had advanced to a secondary school let alone a university. Understandably my parents were anxious that I should get a safe and respectable job, in a bank or office perhaps, and as soon as possible. My father was a wonderful man, utterly unselfish, very hard working and devoted to his wife and son, but he was doubtful about the practical benefits of staying on at school. But my mother, a very strong personality, had the nerve and confidence in me to let me continue in higher education (and with two years added for national service) until I eventually embarked on a career which seemed to justify the enormous sacrifices they had made on my behalf.

Although I obtained a good degree at Oxford University, it would have seemed highly unlikely, well into my twenties, that I could become an academic historian, and impossible that I would specialise in military history since there were no positions for which I could apply.

It is a very common experience, of course, for young people to have to struggle and endure many disappointments in achieving their ambitions, particularly when there are few opportunities and the qualifications necessary are unclear. I can only hope that the details of my own career are sufficiently interesting to recount. On a broader view I certainly lived through a period that witnessed a remarkable expansion and refinement of military history as studied in universities. I am proud of the modest role I played in that development.

1

A Wartime Childhood

I was born in April 1936 so my pre-war memories are perhaps tinged with a rosy glow of hindsight. I lived in the gatehouse to a big estate, as I do now, which was requisitioned by the Army on the outbreak of war. My father continued as the gardener until conscripted, and for a while my parents acted as caretakers at Beechwood House, until the officers mess was organised. My mother spoke warmly of the Commandant, Colonel Foot, but it was not until 2005 that I stumbled on a remarkable coincidence when I asked the distinguished historian of S.O.E, M.R.D. Foot if he was related to the Colonel Foot of my childhood. Not only was Richard Foot his father but he, Michael, had visited Beechwood at weekends from Oxford and had slept in a tent on the lawn while the sites for the guns and searchlights of Anti-Aircraft Command were selected. He may well have seen me in my pedal car on the forecourt, though in his memoirs he adds seven years to my age.

Consequently I grew up with the Army literally close to our front door. Nissen huts sprang up alongside the drive which my father had tended so thoroughly, and there was an endless flow of lorries, one of which ran right over me without doing any harm. A poignant memory is of soldiers kicking a football about in the autumn dusk while a nearby gramophone played Cole Porter's 'Night and Day'.

Like most small children I hated gas masks and soon disposed of mine. In the spring of 1940 I witnessed the roads being dug up for tank traps, sign posts twisted or blacked out and the larger fields cluttered with rusting farm machinery. Then there came the frequent whining sound of air raid warnings followed by the more soothing all-clears. I believe I heard the ominous drone of some of the Luftwaffe attacks on London, and I'm sure I later saw the glow of the capital burning from our vantage point on the Chiltern Hills west of Marlow. The nearest the war came to us was the autumn of 1940 when the enemy jettisoned his bombs along the Thames Valley, cratering the fields and leaving dangerous holes for swimmers. On 27 October a bomb fell on the back of my maternal grandmother's cottage in nearby Medmenham causing her great shock and leaving a large crater with an alarming gash in the outside lavatory.

My father, born in November 1901, was nearly too old for military service, but he was eventually conscripted and served for most of the war as an ordinary airman in the RAF Regiment. He was moved frequently, guarding bitterly cold airfields on the north coast and travelling overseas for the only time in his life – to the Isle of Man. I believe he saw some terrible sights, such as rear gunners being hosed out of their cockpits, but he never talked about these missing years. Like so many of the hard times in his life, he endured the war years stoically, making a few lasting friends and waiting the longed-for return to his wife and son.

There were only a few books in our house (novels by HG Wells and Arnold Bennett I recall), but the only ones I read as a child were about birds. For a few years I was an avid reader of comics, such as the *Hotspur* and the *Rover*, but never the *Beano* or *Dandy*, though the latter proved to be the staple intellectual fare of my bombardier during basic training. From the comics and the radio my mother and I absorbed notions of our armed forces' heroic actions in a struggle which Britain and the Dominions were bound to win in the end. The first non-British troops I encountered were Canadians, who dug trenches near a house where my mother was working. I invited a dozen or so in for tea and was rewarded with a red hackle, but it was far from being my finest hour.

With a few other boys I 'played at soldiers', devising elaborate commando games. At an early age I was taken to the nearby 'trenches' at Marlow Common, some twenty acres of a practice network dug during the First World War and still clearly visible today. Only recently did I learn that Harold Macmillan had trained there as a Grenadier Guards subaltern while staying at Court Gardens in Marlow.

As already remarked, I can lay no claims to have been a precocious student of military history. Two childhood favourites did make a lasting impression, however, and testify to an early interest in warfare, and particularly, in battles. On Sunday afternoons my father and I would cycle a few miles to his parents' house in Frieth. In a window alcove, always in memory redolent with the scent of geraniums, I would become absorbed in looking at the illustrations in the first two massive volumes of *With the Flag to Pretoria*. I must have gained early knowledge of the 'Black Week' of British defeats in 1899, and the opposing leaders: Roberts and Kitchener versus Kruger and Cronje. But the picture that sticks in the memory is the artist's impression of the young Winston Churchill, on the run from his Boer captors, hiding amid rocks and watched by a hopeful vulture. These, and the third volume, I kept until recently when they were ruined by flooding.

The other volume, which I still cherish, is *The Red Book of British Battles* published soon after the outbreak of war in 1914 and given to my father by his sister Winn as a birthday present. As Herbert Strang proclaimed in his Preface "The present time, when our country is engaged in the most gigantic struggle in its history … offers an occasion for reminding the boys of the Empire of some of the great battles of the past." The vividly illustrated battles from Blenheim to Omdurman could easily, in the imagination, be updated to Dunkirk, El Alamein and Normandy.

Until recently I could remember my teachers' names, and those of the boys and girls in adjacent desks, at my primary schools in Marlow between 1941 and 1945, but these years were clouded by poor health, including TB of the neck gland, which was diagnosed and removed just in time. Despite missing a year with this illness I passed the eleven-plus exam and was very fortunate to go to an excellent grammar school, Sir William Borlase's Marlow (1624), then single-sex but long since mixed, much larger but still with an outstanding reputation.

Unlike many authors and artists, who look on their school days with anguish, I enjoyed my seven years at Borlase immensely. I was naturally good at games (cricket, rugby, athletics) and good at the subjects which interested me without acquiring the dreaded label of 'swot'. It was a special privilege, which I did appreciate at the time, to spend three years in the sixth form housed in the old library and seated, not at desks, but at a grand, polished table with leather-bound chairs. Even more fortunate I had three or four close friends who did a lot to stimulate and encourage each other. We were remarkably widely read in English literature and foreign literature in translation, particularly the great Russian novelists and playwrights. Here I am pleased to pay tribute to the inspiration of an outstanding teacher of English,

Charles Davenport, to whom I owe the transformation from a somewhat narrow focus on sport to the sudden realisation (at the age of fourteen) that literature could be exciting for its own sake, whether or not it was a topic for examination. Being an only child with doting parents was doubtless a great asset compared to some of my classmates.

Our history master, by contrast, was sound and competent but dour and uninspiring. He seldom smiled and I never recall him laughing. He once criticised me as a 'wordy beggar' for presenting an essay on the French Revolution in the style of Thomas Carlyle. J.C. 'Junk' Davies was a wounded veteran of the First World War so he was deserving of the understanding that schoolboys rarely show. His own experience had put him off the study of war and this was reflected in his style of teaching. He provided a bare summary of campaigns and peace treaties and, as far as I remember, ended his course at the outbreak of war in 1914. Not surprisingly I did much better at English than History (with French and Latin as complementary A level subjects) and should perhaps have opted for the former at Oxford. However I was strongly advised not to read English because Anglo-Saxon was compulsory and my main areas of interest, the Romantic period (especially Hazlitt, de Quincey and Wordsworth), and modern novels (E.M. Forster, Virginia Woolf, D.H. Lawrence and James Joyce) were unlikely to be on the syllabus. Thus, when I left school aged 18 in 1954, I had no ambition to be an academic, and would have derided any suggestion that I might one day teach and write military history.

I served for precisely two years (1954–6) in the Royal Artillery in the ranks of gunner, lance bombardier and second lieutenant. Had I known at the time that I would become a military historian I might have taken the experience more seriously, but being sure of a place at Worcester College Oxford inclined me to count the days to demob and to get by with a minimum of effort. Much of the routine on the path to a commission was unavoidably tedious; there was no way in which dismantling and re-assembling a Bofors' breech-block in icy conditions could be made enjoyable, and the lectures on map reading and regimental history could be dull and even farcical. But I enjoyed all the physical activities, apart from compulsory boxing. There was a certain amount of bullying during basic training, particularly against the minority with 'school certs' (only 6 out of 90 in my intake at Albany Barracks at Parkhurst on the Isle of Wight), but my prowess at games saved me from any ill treatment.

Life was infinitely more enjoyable as an officer in Germany where I served in 12th Light Anti-Aircraft Regiment, a component of 7th Armoured Brigade so I could proudly wear the insignia of the Desert Rats. I was stationed briefly at the enchanting, snow-covered town of Celle, and then moved to the more industrialised area of Herford. At the latter I lived in a chummery in the town, sharing a batman with another Oxford-bound subaltern, David Weight. Apart from the annual camp for firing practice on the Baltic coast near Kiel there was plenty of leisure. I played cricket and football for the regiment and took my time in learning to drive (obligatory for officers) in the beautiful country in the Weser Valley around Minden.

There was a certain amount of hostility between national service officers and the short-service regulars who understandably resented our laid-back and in some cases condescending attitudes. I was the accidental cause of an open fight between the two factions when I wore a PT vest under my blues instead of the compulsory starched shirt at a mess dinner. I had forgotten that jackets would be taken off for the silly game of 'high cockalorum' after dinner, and when my 'crime' was exposed I was punched in the face by a regular officer. I fought back and a general mêlée ensued. My assailant broke his thumb, and as I was an opening batsman for the regiment the Adjutant, (and cricket captain), excused me from any extra orderly officer duties.

Although I was keen to start at Oxford I was well aware that this was an exciting and largely carefree interval in my life. In retrospect I appreciated even more that national service had done me a great deal of good. I had mixed with a great variety of young men, especially during basic training, including semi-literates, ex-criminals and many more whose regional accents I could not understand. I had learnt to obey orders, however irrational they might appear, and to issue them, albeit on a very modest level. As a spoilt only child who had never been abroad I had coped with home-sickness and had travelled on leave by myself to Italy. The two year gap in an unintellectual institution enhanced the prospects of more advanced study at university; and the experience of military life, however superficial, would later be useful in my academic career.

2

Oxford

I read Modern History at Worcester College, Oxford between 1956 and 1959. I was enchanted by the College on my first visit: passing through the somewhat forbidding portals one was confronted by a wonderful vista; stately 18th century buildings on the right and a row of mediaeval cottages on the left; immaculate lawns leading to a wall bordering the Provost's garden with a lake beyond. So convinced was I that this was my appointed destiny that I named no other college on my preference list. I duly passed the Common Entrance examinations in December 1953 and never regretted my choice.

Since I make some critical remarks at the end of this section on the lack of encouragement I received later from my tutors, it is right to stress here that I came up with romantic notions of the university derived from literary sources such as Matthew Arnold's *The Scholar Gipsy* and Max Beerbohm's *Zuleika Dobson*, and from J.C. Masterman's splendid history *To Teach the Senators Wisdom*, which I chose as a school prize. Not only did this infatuation survive my three years of residence with the typical problems of failed affairs and the onset of religious doubts (which greatly upset my mother), but endured until quite recently when it was undermined by madding crowds, parking problems, closure of favourite haunts and the loss of personal contacts.

The Oxbridge tutorial system is rightly praised, but inevitably there are flaws and varied experiences. My first elderly college tutor collapsed with some kind of mental breakdown during the first term. He gave us ambiguous essay topics and repeatedly confused me with my colleague Colin Castle. He was replaced by James Campbell, scarcely older than us and rudely nick-named 'Little Jim' who would achieve distinction as a scholar of the Anglo-Saxon period, but did not tutor me. I was farmed out, with fellow Worcester men, to three female dons. Betty Kemp of St Hughes was excellent and helped me to achieve a distinction in constitutional history. Lady Clay was an expert on the Normans, but had the irritating habit of repeatedly interrupting one's reading of essays to anticipate important points which were just about to be made. This led to a stultifying guessing game in which one attempted to forestall these interruptions in advance. Finally, Anne Whiteman at Lady Margaret Hall, was a formidable presence whose special period was early modern Europe, on which my background was weak. She would recommend half a dozen tomes, mostly in French, for the weekly essay (one of two throughout the term), and detect from long experience what you had failed to read. Undergraduettes told me that they would sit up reading through the night trying to complete the list, but I never did this and probably saved myself from a nervous breakdown. I felt more warmly towards Dr Whiteman when I discovered that she had lodged in my home village, Medmenham, during the war while working for the vital Photographic Reconnaissance Unit at nearby Danesfield Mansion. To remind her of those exciting days I took her a bunch of the local bluebells. I did not expect her exacting standards to be modified, nor were they.

Since I was not a Scholar at the College I was not put under pressure to aim for first class honours. My essays were always ready on time and generally of a sound upper second class standard, but I somehow made time for a great deal of sport. I represented the College's first teams at cricket, rugby and soccer, and on some weekends travelled home to play for Marlow at the first two. At one end of term Collection it was noted that I had done quite well academically considering the amount of sport I played, and on another occasion the Provost forestalled criticism by remarking that I had recently played an outstanding game of soccer against Brasenose.

Belatedly I began to hope that I might do well enough in Finals to stay on and do research. This change of mind was mainly due to enthusiasm for the Special Subject which began in the summer term of the second year. I chose the Military History special partly for negative reasons: my Latin was not good enough for the mediaeval topics which interested me, while many of the modern options were concerned with such dreary matters as the industrial revolution, the corn laws and the widening of the franchise.

On the face of it the Military History special did not seem all that appealing either. The prescribed campaign was the Second Coalition against Revolutionary France (1797–1802) based in part on a large volume of documents, and supplemented by study of the works of two theorists, Carl von Clausewitz's *On War* (in the three volume edition), and Julian Corbett's *Some Principles of Maritime Strategy*. Clearly the History Faculty had not yet braced itself to offer a course on the First World War, let alone the Second. The Special Subjects were significant because they were awarded two papers in the Finals.

Military History was taught at All Souls by the Chichele Professor, Norman Gibbs, assisted by Dr Piers Mackesy at Pembroke. Mackesy was writing a series of scholarly but dry volumes on the Napoleonic Wars from which he drew heavily in his lectures. Gibbs, a reserved and rather austere character who eventually published the first volume of the official history of *Grand Strategy in the Second World War*, did not so much lecture as comment in detail on the set texts. Having recently been appointed to a chair then unique in its subject at the age of 43, he seemed to feel under no pressure to publish. Lady Liddell Hart, perhaps jealous because her husband (Basil) had written vastly more on military history without getting this coveted chair, would remark when Gibbs' name was mentioned, that what he really cared about was his rose garden. This was a bit unfair because Gibbs took his teaching duties seriously, especially his doctoral candidates. I do not recall that we received any individual supervision, but he did succeed in arousing my interest in his subject more than my other teachers. The select campaign seemed a bit remote, but being obliged to wrestle with documentary sources was challenging. What really stimulated my imagination however were the strategic ideas of Clausewitz and Corbett which opened up an exciting new way to study military history. I did well in this subject in Finals and began to hope that I could pursue it as a career if only I could get a foot on the lowest rung of the ladder.

Unfortunately I received no encouragement at all from the senior historian at Worcester College, Harry Pitt. Harry had his favourites and I was not one of them. Was his dislike of me due to snobbery over my non-public school background, or perhaps to my propensity to continue arguing in tutorials when I was supposed to listen to his concluding words of wisdom? I recall a tutorial in which my companion, Colin Castle, read out a superficial essay and Pitt suggested he had not read the recommended texts 'Good lord, Harry,' Colin replied, 'I never read more than one book or I get confused.' I would not have dared to be so brazen, but Colin got away with it.

Like my history master at school, Harry Pitt had been soured by his military experience, though of course in the Second World War. He walked with a limp which, it was rumoured, had been caused by falling down the NAAFI steps. Whatever the truth, it became clear that he detested war and military history so that my growing interest in the subject met with increasing hostility. He and James Campbell had evidently decided that my academic ceiling was that of a games-playing schoolteacher. My results in Finals were not good enough to secure a research grant, but I like to think that in their position I would have shown me a little more enthusiasm and encouragement. At the time, however, I had to accept that the college's judgement was tough but reasonable. I had not done well enough to earn a research grant and must try to pursue my ambitions elsewhere. I kept in touch with Harry Pitt for several years and sent him copies of my early publications, but received no positive response and certainly no acknowledgement that I had made good after all. This surly behaviour did leave a bitter memory which rankles to this day.

3

Getting a foot on the ladder, 1959–62

Chance or good fortune play a crucial role in our lives. Even before leaving Oxford I had met the mentor and the research supervisor who between them would transform my prospects and largely determine my career; namely Captain B.H. (later Sir Basil) Liddell Hart and M.E. (later Sir Michael) Howard.

In December 1958 Liddell Hart came to live on the hill above Medmenham about a mile from my parents' cottage near the river. Through my father Basil heard that I was in my third year reading history at Oxford and asked to see me. Our first meeting on 4 January 1959 was truly a turning point in my life. Fortunately I had just read two of his books and was able to say honestly that I had found them very interesting. He was extremely friendly and autographed five of his books for me. For the first time I saw the 'rogues gallery' in his study: a wall covered with portraits including Rommel and other German generals, T.E. Lawrence, Robert Graves, Lloyd George and many others. The signed portrait of Mussolini was less conspicuous on a side table. Basil was clearly willing to help me and I found this first meeting 'very cheering indeed' with 'the hope of a career if I do well enough'.

In the next few weeks Basil read four of my rather ordinary Oxford essays and said they made some interesting points, and in the following months he read several articles in draft, advising me where they might be published. A bit later he even found time to look at my MA thesis on the Cardwell Reforms (1868–74); a subject he was not interested in. Then, and for the rest of his life, he was remarkably generous with his time, given that he was an internationally renowned military historian and critic, who was working hard to finish his *Memoirs* and his long overdue *History of the Second World War*.

While there was still a chance that I might stay on at Oxford to do a B.Litt. Michael Howard, then a young lecturer in History at King's College, London, had suggested that the Cardwell Reforms would make a good subject. They were certainly a neglected topic awaiting a scholarly reappraisal, but I suspect Michael also realised that the later 19th century would put a distance between my work and Basil's dominant interest in the First World War and after. There was no serious friction over my failure to implement some of Basil's marginal suggestions until the mid 1960s when I contributed the chapter on the First World War to the *New Cambridge Modern History* (volume XII) and Basil that on the Second World War. Basil thought that I had been too generous to Haig and Robertson in my draft and urged me to be more critical. I did not do so but realised I must tread warily on topics where I knew he felt strongly. One of the very few occasions on which he displayed anger was when I sent off an article (to *History Today* I think), without first showing it to him.

Nearly all the letters that Basil sent me between 1959 and 1962 were wholly or in part concerned with finding academic employment for me. Re-reading this correspondence after many years I am astonished at the time and trouble he took in trying to help me; a lively and industrious young man, whose father worked part-time as his gardener, but who had not yet published anything of note. It would be tedious to detail all Basil's efforts but the following will convey some sense of his determination to get me onto the academic ladder.

Soon after meeting me he wrote to Harry Pitt and Michael Howard about a research grant. He introduced me to Major-General Hubert Essame who suggested I try for a commission in the Royal Army Education Corps, or go for a job at Southampton University where he had connections. Early in 1961 Basil wrote references for me to Glasgow and Leicester Universities, the latter granted me an interview where I saw the padded cells of the former asylum, but failed to get the job in Victorian Studies (transport not war was the preferred specialism). Basil wrote to his old Cambridge College (Corpus Christi) and also to Pennsylvania State where he had contacts. At his suggestion I also had two meetings with George Brown MP, then deputy leader of the Labour Party. Finally, though it does not include numerous failed applications for research grants, Basil stressed my merits and potential to Dr Roger Morgan, a friend of his at Aberystwyth University, where I duly made the shortlist of four but was unsuccessful because they wanted someone to specialise in contemporary international relations. This proved to be a 'blessing in disguise' as did also the failed interview for a post at Lampeter University where my interest in war clearly dismayed two very senior Welsh churchmen.

The recital of unsuccessful applications and interviews has broken the chronology of my struggle to earn a living after Oxford, but I shall shortly return to Basil's indefatigable efforts which surely did at last bear fruit.

Basil entertained a stream of visitors and made a point of introducing me to them, even if I was working shabbily dressed in the garden. Occasionally I would be invited to lunch where Kathleen attempted to interrupt Basil's flow of talk to ensure that everyone had a chance to speak. More often, while Basil took his afternoon nap, I was left to entertain his guests in the sunny entrance porch or outside under a cherry tree in the courtyard. In this regime there was no excuse for being shy or tongue-tied and frequent practice greatly helped my self-confidence. Among the numerous people I noted meeting were: General Sir Ernest Swinton, Norman Gibbs, General Sir Charles Broad, Theodore (Ted) Ropp (a senior American military historian at Duke University), Arthur Marder, Alun Gwynne-Jones (Lord Chalfont), who came to seek Basil's advice on being appointed defence correspondent of *The Times*, Bernard Levin, Reginald Paget QC and Field Marshal von Rundstedt's grandson.

A memorable challenge was to amuse Major-General J.F.C. ('Boney') Fuller and his Polish-born wife Sonia. I see I noted on 28 August 1960 that we sat outside in the shade and I found him 'a delightful old man', but I also recall his forbidding hawk-like aura and the difficulty of drawing him into conversation. I noted that we talked about the French Army, Sir Arthur Bryant (very critically) and the use of poison gas in warfare. On the last topic he replied that he still favoured its use as a more humane form of warfare. I later wished I had had the courage to press him on his relationship with Sir Oswald Mosley and the Fascist Movement.

Basil had arrived in Medmenham with a huge library and an enormous archive. He quickly distributed his 'working library' in his large study but a large proportion had to be sorted and arranged in converted stables which were reached through a barn. He also had long runs of many journals in English, French and Irish. *The Army Quarterly*, *RUSI Journal*, and *Encounter* were particularly interesting to me. The archive of files, packed in boxes and initially housed in the barn loft, posed a daunting challenge to Kathleen, myself and an American professor, Jay Luvaas, who was preparing his long essay on Basil's work for inclusion in his excellent book *The Education of an Army* (1965). This sorting and re-arranging of books and documents was laborious but also exciting and very useful for me. I could browse as I liked and borrow any book that Basil was not actually working on: sometimes I miscalculated and would receive an urgent call to return the missing item.

Basil was an inveterate hoarder: letters, bills, typed notes and press cuttings were stuffed into files year by year and rarely, if ever, properly sorted and never 'weeded'. For example in the dense files for 1924, amongst many bills, begging letters and routine correspondence, I came across an early letter from Bernard Montgomery which Basil had completely forgotten about. Weeding had to be carried out ruthlessly and in secret from Basil or we should have been overwhelmed by the sheer amount of paper. I was well aware at the time, and have certainly been so ever since, that I was enormously privileged to have unfettered access to this unique collection of military books, journals and documents within walking distance of my home. The archive remained at States House for several years after Basil's death in 1970 until transferred to King's College, London. Above all I was fortunate to have enjoyed a warm friendship with the 'Sage of Medmenham' who would answer questions and offer guidance on all these varied sources, including the authors and personalities he knew so well.

I had numerous relaxed one-to-one conversations with Basil, especially in the late evenings when he had finished his work for the day. I wish I had acted as a Boswell to his Dr Johnson but regrettably I usually only jotted down a heading, such as 'German generals', 'Robert Graves' or 'military reactionaries'. He would talk readily about his non-military interests such as the deeper significance of women's fashions and disparities in the books of the New Testament. I recall him talking late at night about T.E. Lawrence's sexual 'hang ups' and masochism. Once he confided to me his dislike of certain sexual behaviour, but in general I suspect he was rather prim and puritanical, though it must be said that his height and dandified dress style attracted several ladies of a certain age. Basil's impish sense of humour may be illustrated by a remark at lunch (on 23 August 1960) that Bertrand Russell had once argued that cowardice not courage should be inculcated as the prime virtue in the public schools. In a very long discussion on 5 February 1961 he quoted Bismarck's suggestion that if the Dutch and Irish temperaments were swapped the latter would neglect the dykes and be drowned. He opposed capital punishment 'on rational grounds' and believed flogging often acted as a sexual stimulus. He opposed my view that Lloyd George could and should have ousted Haig and said that had he been in office Churchill too could not have acted. Lastly, for now, I recall Basil talking at length (3 August 1959) on a favourite topic of whether wives were an asset, hindrance or neutral in helping their husband's careers. In the armed services he thought the 'hindrance' column – he had made a list from personal knowledge – was the longest (Sonia Fuller being an arch offender) and the 'asset' column being the shortest. In his own case one can confidently state that Kathleen was an asset, though she was only there to help him in the latter part of his career from the mid 1930s. I have tried to show in this section that Basil was remarkably generous in the time and support he offered me. When I once apologised for interrupting him at a particularly difficult time he replied 'I will always have time for you, Brian'.

At this stage in my career I could have been said to be 'walking in Liddell Hart's footsteps' because he had given me a pair of his hand-made shoes, but his feet were too long and narrow for me to wear them. Likewise his expensive suits were too big for me because he was 6 foot 4 inches tall. But for years I did wear his striking ornamental waistcoats. Most bizarrely, when I had to spend several weeks in bed in very hot-weather he gave me two pairs of Hore-Belisha's silk pyjamas – cream with blue trimmings and 'L H-B' embroidered over the heart. This is the closest I have been to sleeping with a Secretary of State for War.

I first met Michael Howard at States House on 1 March 1959 when there was still a chance that I would gain a grant to do research at Oxford. Michael was then only 37 years of age but he seemed older and quite formidable. I always addressed him as 'Sir' until I was told to desist. He had won the Military Cross at Salerno while serving with the Coldstream Guards, whose war-time history he had published in 1951. His interest in current international affairs was attested by his recent publication *Disengagement in Europe* (1958) but he had still to publish his magnum opus *The Franco-Prussian War* (1962). When I first met him Michael was a lecturer in War Studies at King's College, London: he did not yet have a department but was clearly a rising star. It proved to be an ideal time for me to make a favourable impression. When I met him again at States House on 16 August 1959 he decided that I should do research under his supervision, whether or not I received a grant. This was a tremendous boost to my confidence which enabled me to put the rejection at Oxford behind me.

I spent the autumn term teaching at The Cedars School in Leighton Buzzard. I began to learn how to hold the attention of lower form pupils who were not necessarily interested in history. I made virtually no progress on my thesis, but was able to attend some of Michael Howard's military history seminars at the Institute of Historical Research. Here I at once witnessed a higher level of research papers and discussion than anything I had experienced at Oxford. It was a small group of at most a dozen scholars; some had already made a mark such as Peter Paret, M.R.D. Foot and Kenneth Bourne, while the others were beginners like me. I was very impressed by some of the early presentations I heard. An American Paul Guinn, for example, spoke eloquently on British politics and strategy in the First World War and went on to gain his PhD, even though the official documents had not yet all been released by the Public Record Office. Kenneth Bourne, already lecturing at the L.S.E., gave a paper on communications in the American Civil War which was so precise, polished and meticulously documented that even Michael Howard found it hard to pose a searching question. Here was a lesson which I experienced many times when chairing the same seminar later; namely that near-perfect papers did not stimulate the best discussions. Much better to have a flawed paper with loose ends or a provocative argument which could launch a lively discussion. Wherever possible, as I also learnt, it was important to prevent one or two 'experts' on a given topic from dominating the discussion. More diffident scholars had to be persuaded that they too had a voice in an amicable group activity where pursuit of the truth, and encouragement of colleagues, was more important than showing off.

Michael Howard's style as chairman impressed me from the outset. He would write down just three of four points in an immaculate Germanic hand, ensure that these were dealt with in discussion, and sum up in a few judicial sentences. I could never match the precision and clarity of Michael's razor-sharp mind, but in any case preferred to let the discussion ramble a bit, leaving scope for unexpected avenues to be opened up, before concluding with a few sentences on the main points raised, and any key issues which had been neglected.

The job at Leighton Buzzard was for one term only but just in time I secured an appointment for two terms (i.e. January – July 1960) at Reigate Grammar School. I learnt later that there had been forty applicants but the senior history master wanted a competent history teacher who could also play cricket for his local club. This was a good school with a lively sixth form that stretched my knowledge and quick-wittedness, but some of the lower forms, particularly a dreaded second form 'Remove' tested my patience near to breaking point. I would dash off to the IHR Seminar in anticipation of the final bell, risking the headmaster's wrath and once getting a reprimand. I continued to read obsessively but found little time for serious research.

In the autumn of 1960 I at last gave myself some time to work on my thesis. I found lodgings in London with a former school friend, Alan Blair, and supported myself by teaching part-time at a secondary school in Richmond while also running a weekly WEA class in Woking on American literature.

On 17 October I dashed to a tutorial with Michael at his Onslow Square residence and received 'scathing criticism' of both the style and contents of a draft thesis chapter. Among my faults I had mentioned 'withering fire' about which Michael commented coldly 'all fire is withering' – as he knew from personal experience. He expressed 'brutally frank' doubts as to my prospects of becoming a university teacher; the WEA was more in line. I came away feeling very miserable but after so many disappointments I was determined to succeed.

My breakthrough seemed to have come on 24 November when, after a friendly interview at Sandhurst with Brigadier Peter Young, I was offered a place as a lecturer in history, subject to confirmation by the War Office. On the basis of the interview and the confident manner of both Young and the Head of Studies (Anderson) I resigned my two teaching appointments in Richmond and Woking: neither was congenial to me but I needed the money. On 8 December I received a very upsetting ('slimy') letter from Sandhurst saying that there were difficulties with the War Office about my appointment and the offer was withdrawn.

Judging by my diary entries I took this latest disappointment quite calmly, perhaps sensing that I might have had a lucky escape. A job teaching military history to officer cadets had its attractions and the department there has attracted some excellent historians including Chris Duffy, Richard Holmes and John Keegan. But it was not a university and did not offer the challenge of teaching undergraduates, graduates and doctoral candidates. As some of my students who taught there later would discover the military culture could be stifling if they were unsuited by temperament or stayed too long.

So many applications for grants or academic appointments had come to nothing and even the Labour Exchange decided I was not eligible for any money. The position was becoming desperate. My mother was unwell and was worried about my future: she was working herself to death though I did not realise this. Then, at last, I got a foothold on the lowest rung of the academic ladder. On 13 June 1961 I was successful at an interview at Exeter University and awarded a one year Tutorship in History. As the title made clear, this was a strictly limited opportunity for a promising young teacher to gain tutorial experience over a very extended span of history with no lecturing responsibilities. Though it now seems scarcely credible the salary was only £400 for the academic year.

Exeter was a delightful city and I enjoyed my academic duties so much that I asked the head of department, Professor Frank Barlow, if there was any chance of staying on, with a proper salary. There was not. Consequently I had to start looking for a new position almost straight away. I published several articles in journals such as *History Today* and my MA thesis was approved early in 1962. My already turbulent emotional life sunk to its nadir with the sudden death of my mother (aged 59) on 23 February 1962. My devastated father proposed to sell our home and go into lodgings because he could not bear to live there alone. It was imperative that I get a proper job.

At last my perseverance was rewarded; after a friendly interview on 29 May 1962 I was offered a lectureship in history at Liverpool University. I still like to believe that my own merits contributed to my success, but when I later saw the references that Basil had written for me I appreciated that the cards had been stacked in my favour. To an old friend, W. Lyon Blease, formerly Professor of Law at Liverpool University he wrote:

> I have just heard from a young historian, Brian Bond, of whom I have a high opinion, that he is applying for the post of Assistant Lecturer there, so I would like to reinforce this application with my own personal recommendations of him.
>
> Since moving to Medmenham in 1958, when he was in his final year at Oxford, I have had numerous discussions with him, and have been impressed by his ardent interest in history (and military history), his extensive reading, and his historical grasp. I have been still more impressed by the way he has developed in balance and judgment during these years.
>
> He has potentialities for historical research which make it very desirable that he should be given adequate opportunity to pursue it.
>
> I consider him one of the most promising young historians I have come across anywhere.

And to Professor David Quinn, Head of the Department of History:

> Many thanks for your letter of the 10th. I have been particularly impressed by the wideness of Brian Bond's interests compared with most of the other younger men I know who are specializing in the field of military history. That is one of the main reasons why I consider him one of the most promising of the young historians I have come across anywhere. While he has great powers of concentration, he has also a most refreshing intellectual curiosity and the wide background knowledge he has acquired adds much to the value of his studies in the field of military history. That combination in turn has much helped him to infuse the students he is teaching with his own enthusiasm – as I have heard from several sources.
>
> I am confident that he would be well able to 'teach outlines of world history in the past century', and I wish that there were more of his generation who were anything like as well fitted.

As the second reference shows, the main requirement for the lecturer to teach was a new survey course on 'World History since 1850'. There were fifty or more students drawn not only from history, but also from joint degree courses involving politics, economics and geography. In addition I had to teach periods of European history which I had not studied at Oxford, and some British history with which I was more familiar. In retrospect it was extremely useful to have a working knowledge of 'World history', but for the first two years the range of reading required was very demanding, not only for the lectures but also to prepare reading lists which would stretch the keener students. One of the brightest students I taught briefly was Ian Kershaw, then a mediaevalist but now Sir Ian and an outstanding historian of the Third Reich. When I met him decades later at a conference, probably in Potsdam, and reminded him of his undergraduate days, he remembered me not as a teacher but as a formidable tackler, in the Norman Hunter mould, in a staff versus student soccer match.

I was fortunate indeed to gain my first, full academic appointment at a good 'Redbrick University', albeit one still disfigured by Second World War devastation, and with a very strong history department. Most of the staff went out of their way to be helpful to a beginner and I particularly appreciated the friendship of Irene Collins (later President of the Historical Association), John Rowe, Tony Ryan and Philip Bell (whose death has been announced as I check this in February 2017). Naturally quite a lot of military history was covered in my various courses but I was too busy to offer a special subject in the field.

Madeleine (my wife since September 1962), and I were both generally happy in our spacious Victorian flat, in the city and in the easily accessible country in North Wales – especially rambling on the Clwyd hills. But we felt acutely the pull of lonely relatives in the south and hoped we might eventually move back to the London area. The opportunity arose sooner than expected. In 1963 Michael Howard was promoted to a new chair in War Studies with the possibility of creating a small department. As early as April 1965 I was interviewed for a lectureship, but was not surprised when the post was given to Dr Wolf Mendl, ten years senior to me but more importantly an experienced scholar in contemporary international affairs and therefore a better complement to Professor Howard's historical background. There was, however, an encouraging hint that I should be patient and in the next year, 1966, I was appointed Lecturer in War Studies by interview but without competition.

In just four years (1962–6) there had been an almost miraculous transformation in my career prospects, and the position in which I had hardly dared to dream about had become a reality. That was not by any means my only stroke of good fortune. My father had unwittingly let our former home ('Olmeda' where I still live) to anarchists who had done their best to ruin the interior. At last in despair he had put it on the market but, incredibly, after a year it lay unsold and nearly derelict. Consequently in June 1966 Madeleine and I were able to return to a short term mess but with the wonderful prospect of living in Medmenham again and working in the Department of War Studies at King's College, London.

4

The Army League, 1961–2

In the autumn of 1961 I was appointed rapporteur for a Study Group of the Army League whose mission was to publish a report on the kind of young officers required in the 1960s. I am sure I owed this lucky break to Basil, who was a friend of the chairman, General Sir Richard 'Windy' Gale, a ferocious-looking but rather amiable old war horse. The committee included some other impressive names, including General Sir Frederick Morgan (chief planner for *Overlord* until Montgomery replaced him), Sir R.T. Paget MP, Peter Mason the High Master of Manchester Grammar School and Rt Hon John Strachey MP.

My task was to interview a variety of senior figures concerned with the Army and its future leaders and to write three or four draft papers for discussion. Consequently I interviewed, among others, the head masters of Portsmouth Grammar School and Wellington College, the commandant at Aldershot and Colonel George Burnett, commander of the Second Battalion Coldstream Guards. I remember impishly asking the last-named if it would be a good idea to recruit more Jewish officers, to which he replied diplomatically that few Jews would be interested and anyway might not be culturally comfortable with the Guards.

My early drafts were discussed in a House of Commons committee room, at one of which Freddie Morgan took me aside, complimented on my elegant paper but said that I had missed the key point: what young officers needed was simply to 'kill, kill, kill'. Fortunately I did not try to incorporate this advice in my revised paper.

The final committee meeting, a splendid 'do' as I noted, was held at the Grosvenor Hotel in Park Lane. After a superb lunch, wine and liquors circulated freely but I kept sober, assuming I would have to make notes on the discussion. I declined one elderly gentleman's invitation to sit on his knee, while another slid gracefully under the table. Sir Richard Gale and the Secretary, Brigadier J. R. Vernham, struck me as badly the worse for wear, but when I anxiously asked the latter what I should record he chuckled and replied that no one would have a clear recollection of what had been said so I could go away and write whatever I liked. Here was a useful insight into how seemingly unanimous committee decisions might be reached. My revised papers were reviewed at length by Gale and Vernham but the final report *A Challenge to Leadership*, launched over lunch at the Savoy Hotel on 27 March 1962 with Sir John Profumo, Secretary of State for War as the guest of honour, was too anodyne to make much of an impact. The experience had, however, been a useful episode in my hectic 'learning curve'.

5

The Department of War Studies

When I joined the Department of War Studies in September 1966 I knew that it was only a couple of years old, but had little idea of the obstacles Michael Howard had had to overcome. The opposition he had faced was partly due to institutional conservatism, particularly evident at King's, but also to a strong left-liberal hostility to war and to the idea that it was a proper subject to be studied at a university. Michael had had to threaten to resign from the stuffy confines of the King's History Department in order to get his lectureship in War Studies, and overcome further opposition before he was awarded a personal chair and then a department. As he fully explained in *Captain Professor* he had to use all his diplomatic skills and academic contacts to gain full recognition of the new subject with its own Board of Studies in the University. A few years earlier he had discovered that the plain and accurate title of 'Military History' would not be accepted for a new seminar at the Institute of Historical Research and instead had given it a diplomatic gloss as 'Military Organisation and the Great Powers'.

Until 1971 the Department found refuge in Dickensian premises at 154 Strand. The staff consisted of Michael, Wolf Mendl, myself and our secretary, June Walker. Michael's office was on the ground floor while Wolf and I had comfortable rooms above him – much better than we would have to endure for nearly twenty years when transferred to the new Strand building.

The vital point about the Department's profile is that until the early 1990s its intake was composed entirely of graduates. The one year MA course, founded in 1965, constituted the core or flagship of our teaching, but Michael had already attracted several promising MPhil – PhD candidates and their numbers rose rapidly. However, it is equally important to stress that from the outset we offered courses open to undergraduates at all the colleges under the University History Board. Dr Ian Roy of the King's History Department and myself taught an optional survey course on military history from the later 17th century to the Second World War. This provided a natural opening for keen students to take a special subject with us and even to go on to post graduate research. I continued to teach Michael's popular special subject on the Franco-Prussian War for a year or two before offering my own 'Gallipoli' with a bound volume of political and strategic documents I had compiled from the Public Records Office.

Although our quarters at 154 Strand were confined and ramshackle – there was very little room for our own library – its great advantage was that the year's MA candidates (eleven in my first year), could all gather round a large seminar table and form a group identity through regular meetings. When the annual intake exceeded thirty there had to be separate tutorial groups and much of this camaraderie was lost.

Michael did not spell out his conceptions of the meaning of 'War Studies' and how it should be taught, but his teaching and publications soon made this clear to us. From the outset of his own academic career he developed a broad inclusive approach to the study of war, with military history as its bedrock:

> The history of war, I came to realize, was more than the operational history of armed forces. It was the study of entire societies. Only by studying their cultures could one come to understand what it was that they fought about and why they fought in the way that they did. Further, the fact that they did so fight had a reciprocal impact on their social structure. I had to learn not only to think about war in a different way, but also to think about history itself in a different way.

As he modestly concluded, he had not invented the concept of War and Society but had done a good deal to popularise it. I would only add the obvious gloss that Michael approached this huge subject from the standpoint of a military historian, whereas at the Open University Arthur Marwick would make an enormous contribution to the subject from that of a social historian.

Although military history constituted the key course in our MA in War Studies which all candidates, some reluctantly, had to take and pass, Michael's ideal of including important associated disciplines such as military sociology, the laws and ethics of war, economics and (I would add though not on his agenda) war literature. At all levels of teaching the subject at university, and more specifically at King's, Michael urged us to avoid two temptations: first to keep the broad picture of 'war and society' in mind and not to become embroiled in technical and tactical detail which could easily lapse into antiquarianism; and secondly to maintain academic standards of objectivity in the quest for historical truth. We were not to be 'pro' or 'anti' war, and it was not our mission to train serving officers with a view to improving their professional skills. This last point caused occasional disquiet and disbelief in some foreign officer candidates as I shall hope to illustrate later.

Having got the Department on its feet and flourishing Michael left us in rather bizarre circumstances which I hope neither he nor his successor, Professor Laurence Martin, will mind me recounting now. Michael called 'the team' i.e. Wolf, June Walker and myself, together in his office and told us he would be leaving at the end of the summer term (1968) because he had been offered a Defence Scholarship at All Souls College, Oxford. Shortly afterwards we were recalled and told that he was staying because the position had been offered to Laurence Martin. Finally, on the third summons, we were told that Laurence Martin had declined the offer so that he, Michael, would be going after all.

The friendly and even 'cosy' atmosphere in the Department was not disturbed by the advent of a new head. Quite the contrary, Laurie's nine year tenure proved a relatively tranquil and enjoyable time. This was partly due to the fact that expansion of student and staff numbers was steady rather than hectic, and clear teaching schedules and routines had been established after the inevitable teething troubles in 1966–8. Without intending any adverse comparison it is fair to say that Laurie was much more interested in contemporary international affairs than military history and so left the historians to run their own show. It amused me that when he chaired the military history research seminar Laurie would try to work 'NATO' into the discussion, whatever the subject of the papers. The only personal consequence of Michael's departure was that I took over his undergraduate Special Subject and several of his PhD candidates. It entailed quite a lot of extra work but since some of them, like John Gooch, were outstanding, it was a privilege to round off what Michael had initiated.

Wolf Mendl was ten year older than me and one year senior to me in the Department. For several years we worked closely together in jointly interviewing most MA and MPhil candidates. I respected his academic expertise and judgement but our characters and interests were so different that we were never close friends. In particular Wolf was a Quaker concerned with contemporary international affairs, whereas I was a military historian who took a Clausewitzian view of the crucial role of war in the evolution of nation states. I am sure Wolf carried out his Departmental duties conscientiously, but he did little to enhance the Department's wider reputation. This was a serious drawback when he acted as head of department between 1978 and 1982 and when vigorous leadership was required. Instead he concentrated on his administrative duties and cut back on his teaching commitments. This did not affect me personally but Michael Dockrill had to take on topics which were not congenial to him. Wolf stayed on until retirement in about 1990, his last years sadly affected by failing eyesight.

Barrie Paskins joined the Department in 1971 as a Defence Fellow whose main duty was to lecture on the ethics of war. His doctorate at Cambridge had been supervised by Bernard Williams, sometime husband of Shirley, the destroyer of Grammar schools. Barrie's political outlook and mine were poles apart, so much so that at one departmental conference I suggested he would be happier living in the Soviet Union. However as an individual I liked him a lot and always found him interesting to talk to, particularly on war poetry and literature where we had more in common. I also admired his lecturing style where, from a seemingly simple opening, he could develop a complicated argument without notes – a risk I seldom took. Towards the end of my term in the Department I served as assessor for some of my colleagues' teaching abilities as judged in anonymous student reports. I was angry to find that some of these were very critical of Barrie on the grounds that he was difficult and even unintelligible. I refused to endorse these criticisms because I believed they were really an indictment of their authors. Whether Barrie would have been happier in a Philosophy Department I cannot say, but he certainly played an important role in War Studies.

Michael Dockrill also joined the Department in 1971 recruited, rather as Michael Howard recruited me, by Laurie Martin, in whose department he had taught at Aberystwyth. Mike Dockrill had earned his PhD at the London School of Economics where his main area of expertise was British foreign policy in the 20th century. Although he did not join us as a military historian he at once took up the challenge and, with me, took an equal share of the heavy teaching duties at BA, MA and PhD levels until we both retired in 2001. Mike seldom complained when asked to take on new subjects, such as air power and air operations, at short notice. He was a popular lecturer and tutor, who was much more willing than I was to socialise with students. In sum, Mike was not only a reliable colleague but also a true friend, as he remains to this day. In 2016 we held a joint party at King's to commemorate our both reaching the age of eighty. The high attendance and warm expressions of affection by former colleagues and students suggested that our efforts had not been forgotten.

Wolf Mendl was head of the Department of War Studies between 1978 and 1982 but was not awarded a chair. At a time when the College was under acute financial pressure the Principal and Council decided that the small Department of War Studies was vulnerable and in need of more vigorous leadership. The chair was advertised and by coincidence the Chichele Professorship of the History of War at All Souls College, Oxford became vacant at the same time. As a Reader in Military History with a good record in teaching and publications I thought I might be a contender for either but of course did not count my chickens. I was disappointed not even to make the short list for Oxford but, in characteristically unpredictable style, that university interviewed two candidates and appointed neither. After a considerable interregnum the distinguished Australian soldier and scholar, Robert J. O'Neill was persuaded to take the chair.

I did make the short list of four for the King's chair but experienced a humiliating interview when only one member of the panel, the late James Joll, asked me a question within my field of competence, the remainder relating to the expansion of contemporary strategic studies. That evening the Principal, Air Marshal Sir Neil Cameron, telephoned to tell me that Lawrence Freedman had been appointed and to ask whether I would stay on under his direction. My answer was of course positive; I was content with my role in the Department and had no thought of 'throwing my toys out of the pram'.

In the event Lawrie Freedman behaved tactfully and considerately, taking a year or two to 'play himself in' before introducing dramatic changes, and even then making no attempt to interfere in the teaching of military history.

Within the next decade or so the Department underwent a transformation with Lawrie displaying energy, vision and ambition in our development which I could not have emulated. Our intake of MA and PhD candidates (many attracted by Lawrie's reputation) increased rapidly with staff numbers growing in proportion. New specialists were appointed in military sociology, Middle and Far Eastern studies and various aspects of contemporary strategic studies and international relations. Not all of these appointments proved to be good team players and I recall some heated exchanges at staff meetings and at the MA Exam Board, over which I had long presided in quieter times. A few junior staff members moved on and, as far as I was concerned, harmony was restored.

Lawrie carried through two very significant innovations in the 1980s in addition to the internal expansion mentioned above. A Centre for Defence Studies was set up nearby on the Strand with its own staff and programmes though closely related to the Department. Even more ambitious, the Department took over the academic teaching programmes at the Service Staff Colleges at Greenwich, Camberley and Bracknell, all three being eventually brought together at the former Royal Military College of Science near Shrivenham in Wiltshire. The academic staff of the new institution were formally recognised as affiliated members of the Department of War Studies. This created a huge outlying empire with the Strand campus at its heart.

In the early 1990s, the College came under severe pressure to expand its undergraduate component, both to strengthen its profile and to bring in vital additional funding. Without a great deal of debate, as I recall, the Department decided to introduce its own three year course leading to a BA in War Studies. I had tended to agree with Michael Howard that it was too early for undergraduates to concentrate entirely on this subject, but the change was accepted with the proviso that entrants should be strictly limited at first and only gradually increased to about thirty per annum, entailing of course that after three years ninety or more undergraduates would require teachers, lecture and seminar rooms, and library facilities. As might have been predicted, this new BA course proved extremely popular with the result that the annual intake soon exceeded the bounds set by the cautious founders.

This vast expansion did not affect me greatly but the pressure to find lecture rooms did prove extremely difficult. Not to mince words it was a nightmare. I was interrupted several times mid lecture because the room had been double booked. By the time I retired in 2001 colleagues had no option but to teach through the lunch hour and well into the evening, perhaps leaving after 7pm for their commute home. Survivors of those happier times, before the introduction of the BA in War Studies, tell me that the situation is now far worse, in terms of numbers, due to the high increase in MA candidates as well. Although I was sorry to be compulsorily retired when I reached the age of sixty-five, it is now a great consolation to me, especially on dark winter mornings, to contemplate the enormous teaching and administrative burdens borne by my successors.

I will write a little more of my teaching experience in what must now be regarded as the halcyon era of the 1970s and 1980s. Although I enjoyed delivering the separate annual lecture courses to BA and MA candidates, the latter focussing less on warfare and more on military theorists. I increasingly found more satisfaction in the smaller seminars which the students had opted for and therefore could be assumed to have a strong commitment.

At the undergraduate level my special subject for many years was 'British Military Policy and Strategy from Munich to the Fall of France'. This was taught chronologically and in great detail, underpinned by a volume of documents (in English and French), from which was drawn a compulsory exam question in each of the two papers. Most students, after an initial shock at the amount of reading required, threw themselves into the enterprise with the satisfactory outcome that they felt themselves to be true masters of the subject by the end. Eight or nine was the ideal number for each student to read one essay in class per term. I sought to bring in a veteran of the operations occasionally to impress on them what it had been like, including Lord Bridgeman, who had taken orders directly from Lord Gort at critical moments, and a Grenadier Guards officer, Sir Peter Thorne, who had been left for dead at Dunkirk but rescued in the nick of time. One student, Robin Brodhurst, was deeply impressed by these visitors, perhaps because he was a former Greenjacket like Bridgeman, and remains a friend to this day. At least one student on this course, (Guy Esnouf), went on to earn a PhD in the Department and several went on to take the MA.

I offered several MA special options but cannot remember them all. In the early days I recall teaching civil-military relations in the First World War and later 'The Face of Battle' following John Keegan's famous book of that title, but concentrating on the problems of conveying 'the truth' about what really happened in combat, given the bland summaries and distortions in many histories. George Macdonald Fraser's *Quartered Safe Out Here* was a brilliant case study of the gulf between what he had experienced in Burma and the sanitised versions he encountered in some of the accounts of authors without first-hand knowledge of the terrain and the enemy.

The MA special which I taught towards the end of my career and enjoyed most was on First World War Memoirs, including French and German examples as well as British, American and Canadian. I delighted in this subject because it combined my love of history and literature; veterans such as Edmund Blunden, Robert Graves and Frederic Manning were first class writers in any company. An important objective in this course was to show the great variety in the authors' attitude to the war and how their experiences were modified by post-war reflections. Contrary to popular notions that they were all merchants of 'gloom and doom' many, like Charles Carrington, remained steadfast in their war-time patriotism while others, such as John (later Lord) Reith and Alfred Pollard VC were unapologetic 'fire-eaters'. I drew heavily on this course, with the valuable input of students in essays and discussions, to write my book *Survivors of a Kind* (2008), which I enjoyed writing because of the wonderful characters selected and their brilliant recreation of their combat experience. The book did quite well but, so far as I know, did not inspire new interest in war memoirs as a comparatively neglected genre.

From the time when Michael Howard bequeathed me some of his PhD candidates in 1968 I seldom had fewer than a dozen in varying states of progress. Some, like David French and Gary Sheffield, knew precisely what they wanted to do and only needed an occasional word of encouragement, while others struggled with defining their topic or with its presentation. One of the greatest dangers in my experience was the tendency to amass a vast amount of research material without thinking how it could be deployed.

I supervised more than fifty successful doctoral theses and am proud that not a single candidate who got as far as the oral examination failed. The topics covered ranged in time from Victorian War Correspondents to the Joint Chiefs of Staff in the Second World War, but with the majority concentrated in the period 1900–45. I was not deeply acquainted with some of the topics but had to read sufficiently widely to be able to spot omissions and offer guidance. I enjoyed good relations with most of my doctoral students and several, like Gary Sheffield, Halik Kochanski and Tony Hampshire remain firm friends. Some gave up because they lacked sufficient leisure or money, others for want of determination. I should be deeply dismayed if any of my PhD candidates felt the need to show their draft chapters to other dons because I was not giving them sufficient feedback. One or two of the late Professor D.C. Watt's students asked me to read some of their work because his curt comments left them in doubt as to whether their progress was satisfactory. I was able to reassure them and recently heard from one, a Canadian Robert Young, who became a professor himself, saying how grateful he was that I had saved him from a crisis of confidence some thirty years ago.

My own progress up the academic ladder was somewhat slow because in a department of five there was not room for more than one Reader, and Wolf Mendl already held that rank. I was eventually appointed Reader in 1977 and awarded a personal chair in 1986. Just before the latter was confirmed I received a tempting offer from Princeton University, initially for one year but with possibility of permanence. Unfortunately I was required to make a snap decision without the possibility of visiting the Department to see if the terms were mutually agreeable. I was apprehensive that if I returned after one year my promotion at King's would be delayed or even 'kicked into the long grass', and besides there were strong domestic reasons for staying in England. I consequently declined an invitation which would surely have drastically changed my life, but have no regrets about my decision. My favourite American author, Henry David Thoreau, proudly declared that he had 'travelled widely in Concord' (Massachusetts), and I have lived with comparable contentment in Medmenham.

My career at King's College ended with gratifying marks of recognition. I was elected a Fellow of the College (FKC) in 1996 and entered *Who's Who* in the same year. I gave the Liddell Hart Lecture to a packed audience in the great hall in the following year. In 2000 I was a Visiting Fellow at All Souls College, Oxford where I prepared the Lees Knowles Lectures delivered in Cambridge later that year. My farewell lecture at King's in 2001 was well-attended although staged on the wrong side of the river due to building work in the Strand campus. I was particularly pleased that Lawrie Freedman was present, thereby putting off an invitation to visit the United States. This account must end on a note of disappointment. I had hoped to continue teaching part-time for a few years and presented several suggestions to make this viable, such as serving as a senior research fellow in the Department or in the Liddell Hart Centre for Military Archives. None of them was accepted and I immediately found that 'goodbye' did mean precisely that and not just 'au revoir'.

6

The Military History Seminar at the Institute of Historical Research

Of all my teaching experiences the format I enjoyed most, whether organising, chairing or simply attending was the seminar in military history at the Institute of Historical Research. It is also the fortnightly event which I miss most in retirement. I had attended this seminar in its early years as a part-time research student in 1959–61, but when I returned as a lecturer five years later the attendance had considerably increased and the meetings were now held in the International Relations Room (now oddly re-styled as the Germany Room).

When Michael Howard left for Oxford in 1968 Laurie Martin ran the seminar for a time, searching for possible links to contemporary issues even in remote paper topics such as the Zulu wars. Donald Cameron Watt also chaired occasionally in a remarkable performance, when he appeared to be catching up on lost sleep, with his head sinking lower and lower until it seemed certain to hit the table. Then, miraculously, when the paper ended, he would rouse himself and make penetrating comments, quite often even severe criticisms. How, we wondered, could he absorb the main arguments in a complex paper while apparently asleep? The puzzle was never solved but occasionally I felt he had missed important points in the presentation and unfairly criticised the speaker as a result. At any rate the Watt method is not recommended. On one occasion I saw him fall asleep right across an elderly American whose son was giving a public lecture.

I became the principal organiser and chairman from about 1970 until I retired on reaching the obligatory age of retirement in 2006. Of course Michael Dockrill, David French, and others were equally competent replacements when I was absent, but I enjoyed attending whenever possible.

After a leisurely tea in the Common Room, where the discussion was always lively and just occasionally better than what followed upstairs, the seminar began promptly at 5.0 with late comers sometimes hard pressed to find a seat. It became a seminar convention that papers should not take more than an hour to deliver at most so that a full discussion could be held for about three quarters of an hour. I noticed over many years that after everyone who wanted to speak had had a chance to do so there would be a lull in which the chairman could take charge, sum up, thank the speaker and conclude. If this climatic point was missed someone was likely to pop up and start more proverbial hares running. Whether this strict time-keeping was universally approved I cannot say, but I often experienced the irritation and ennui in other seminars, dare one say, particularly where French speakers were involved, when the paper and the discussion were allowed to drag on interminably.

Speculating as to why this particular seminar was so successful and popular I concluded that continuous use of the same room at the same time over many decades was a contributory factor as was also its modest size: A densely-packed audience created a better atmosphere than one in a larger space – as we discovered when obliged to meet in a lecture room. But most important, I believe, was the reputation created over many years for high-quality papers, sometimes but not invariably given by experienced speakers, followed by a high standard of discussion. With rare exceptions the tone of meetings was critical but friendly; the aim being to explore the topic as widely as possible and, where appropriate, encourage rather than undermine the speaker's confidence, particularly when a new research topic was being aired. Usually there would be one or two of the latter (out of five in the term) with the rest given by established and sometimes notable scholars such as A.J.P. Taylor, Michael Howard, and Donald Schurman. It was a mark of the seminar's high reputation that invitations to present a paper were rarely refused. Over all the years of my stewardship only one speaker completely failed to turn up, while two others went to King's College by mistake. Perhaps the feature of the seminar that gave me the greatest satisfaction was that several regulars who had attained their doctorates continued to attend for many years out of sheer interest and comradeship. The same was true of other scholars resident in or near London, or visiting foreigners engaged in research. One benefit of this continuity was that the chairman could nearly always call on reliable seniors to open the discussion or revive one that was faltering. I immediately think of Nick Evans, John Peaty and Philip Bell (who, alas, has recently passed on), but there were many others.

Lest the above paragraphs seem unduly complacent it must be admitted that there were embarrassing occasions and a few outright disasters. Among the latter I can recall a very detailed tactical discussion of the Russo-Finnish War of 1939–40 without a single map, and a very long and tedious tirade against the Sykes-Picot Treaty of 1916. Denis Winter brought along both his elderly parents without prior notice; their proud, parental presence severely inhibited discussion. Two of my American friends, Professors John Hattendorf and Williamson ('Bomber') Murray misunderstood my coded advice that papers should not be too long by showing up with virtually no papers at all. The usually prolix Murray spoke for only ten minutes on blitzkrieg, while John Hattendorf thought we could improvise a discussion with no paper at all; quite possible on some topics but not on the little-known 18th century naval subject which he was just beginning to explore. At the other extreme, the longest paper I recorded, on 1 November 1988, was one hour and twenty-eight minutes by a New Zealander, Christine Goulter on 'Coastal Command'. I hope for the sake of the audience that this record still stands. It is with no pleasure that I recall the two female speakers who broke down with nerves, one fleeing the room and having to be rescued, and the other repeating her introductory notes until I had to intervene and try to improvise on what was probably meant to follow. Like me, the audience was deeply sympathetic in both cases and did all that was possible to restore the speakers' confidence.

Over the years several 'oddballs' or eccentrics provided novelty to our proceedings. In Michael Howard's time I recall a fervent and perhaps demented Israel officer-student plunging a dagger into the table under Michael's nose to prove a point. The chairman was not amused. I experienced nothing so startling but we had an occasional mysterious attender who called himself 'Count Grandi' though I don't think he was the son of Dino, Count Grandi, Italian Ambassador in London 1932–9, because he once wore a Guards tie. On one occasion I asked him about a stag's head pattern on his tie and he replied that it was his hunting club. Where do you hunt I asked? On my estates in France he replied. I wish I could remember his eccentric questions or, more often, rambling reflections, which tended to derail the discussion. An example might be that in a broad discussion of strategy in the era of the French Revolution he might interject with a learned disquisition on the origins of drill and marching in step, concluding that the French were bound to win because their pace was more rapid.

To end on a elegiac note: on what was probably the last IHR seminar I shall ever attend I heard an excellent talk by one of my former PhD students, John Peaty on projected but un-made films about T.E. Lawrence long before David Lean's epic starring Peter O'Toole was even thought of. Pushing through the rush-hour crowds to the tube station at Euston Square and thence to the train at Marylebone I reflected, as often before, that these successful meetings fully justified my decision to 'scorn delights and live laborious days' as a university teacher of military history.

7

The British Commission for Military History

I was the president of BCMH from 1986 to 2006, succeeding Dr David Chandler, for many years head of the military history department at Sandhurst. David, noted for his mammoth book on Napoleon, whose persona seems to have influenced him, had taken BCMH into the International Commission in about 1970, long before I had even heard of it. To his credit he had succeeded, where I was to fail, in staging one of the international annual conferences in Britain, having privileged access to an ideal venue at Sandhurst.

David had many good qualities, including a passion for military history, and later he would display great courage in carrying on his work after suffering a crippling stroke. But he was also a tremendous egoist who seemed to regard BCMH as a personal fief; the membership was small and meetings irregular. David would attend all the international conferences as his right even when there were better qualified members who could have been invited to deliver a paper. Dissatisfaction grew to the extent that a small group, I think Dr Ian Roy and Professor Geoffrey Best were among them, visited me at King's and asked if I would take over. I agreed to do so and David was persuaded to step down, thus avoiding what would have amounted to a vote of no confidence. To his credit David continued to attend meetings to the end of his life, but he clearly resented his supersession and was quick to criticise any error, no matter how trivial, which related to matters in the international body's regulations or in our own procedures.

From the outset my main concerns were to raise academic standards in our conferences and to ensure that, in expanding our membership, all newcomers should have something to contribute rather than simply turn up for entertainment. As a corollary, the range of scholarly interests needed to be widened so that we could gradually recruit qualified speakers on virtually any aspect of mediaeval or modern warfare. This ideal did not, however, result in a sudden surge in numbers because it was broadly agreed that meetings should be held in a friendly 'seminar' environment rather than in large conference halls.

In practical organisational terms there was a great deal to be done. I gave the lead as far as possible but of course had many invaluable helpers. The secretary (or 'secretary-general' as the international commission styled the position) was the president's key assistant, not least in insuring that notice of meetings with full, accurate details were sent to all members in good time. Too obvious to need mentioning you may think, but we all know of cases where this was not done. To give just one personal example, I once travelled to Cardiff to give a Historical Association lecture and addressed about six people in a vast hall because the secretary had not sent out invitations.

I was fortunate indeed to have excellent secretaries in Peter Simkins and Gary Sheffield in the hectic early years when just about every aspect had to be introduced or reformed. In addition to overhauling the membership, we had to establish a system of regular meetings in reliable venues; and a fixed time of year for an annual general meeting with a proper audit. A small and very active committee was set up including a finance officer and a liaison officer with the international commission. I chaired nearly all these meetings, often held near the Imperial War Museum. Eventually, after protracted discussion, we drew up a constitution which could be added to or amended at the A.G.M. An annual battlefield tour was introduced from the early 1990s efficiently organised for some years by Nigel and Martine DeLee, both then employed at Sandhurst. After the first, somewhat experimental tour to Normandy, we visited Arras and the Somme before becoming more adventurous. It hardly needs to be spelt out, but this innovation clearly demanded a great deal of planning and sheer hard work. Since I was merely the originator I can say without boasting that this has proved to be an enduring and very popular innovation.

So far as I can recall there were no BCMH publications in the Chandler era. We started in a modest way with glossy brochures for our battlefield tours before publishing a few volumes of our conference proceedings, including *Look to Your Front* (1999) on the First World War and *The Battle for France and Flanders, Sixty Years On* (2001). I regret to report that these volumes were very difficult to edit and not popular with publishers because the contents were by 'divers hands'. I recall my problems with the latter volume in which one contributor's footnotes were more extensive than anyone else's essay, and I was harangued by the publisher for failing to meet his deadline with only about four satisfactory contributions in, and standing in several inches of flood water when answering the phone. There was no sympathy at all for my predicament. One might amend the adage to read 'Don't work with children, animals or other authors' if you need a smooth operation and punctual delivery.

The attempt to publish our own books speedily morphed into a much more manageable journal, for many years entitled *Clio*, but recently up-graded to a first rate academic publication – *British Journal for Military History.*

As mentioned earlier, we felt it to be important to send at least one representative to every international conference, but travel costs were a problem; the venues could be very distant, and qualified speakers could not always get the time off work. I noticed that Americans attending conferences in Europe tended to make them into large-scale family holidays. This was one of the difficulties, including entertainments for families, together with the venue and transport, which ruled out holding a conference in England. Many other countries were subsidised by their defence ministries but our overtures were rejected which at least absolved us from having to dance to the piper's tune.

I attended several conferences as President of BCMH, including Bucharest, Stockholm and Prague, the last-named memorable for the shock announcement of Princess Diana's death. Plunging from tragedy to bathos, it was also at Prague that a Japanese delegate told me 'You big in the world, but you *very big* in Japan.' This meant that my book *The Pursuit of Victory*, was selling well in translation, but since I never received a single yen in royalties I was not impressed.

There was one particular clause in the regulations for these conferences that put me off attending more often. Each national commission could nominate at least one delegate with the right to deliver a paper. The awful result can be imagined. At a conference on the Thirty Years War, for example, I chaired a session with three non-European speakers who had no real interest in that conflict. At another conference on War and Nationalism the speakers on my panel simply narrated a chronological account of wars in their nations without a theme or analysis. There were of course exceptions, but I retain the impression that these conferences were regarded first and foremost as jolly get-togethers for the commission's bureaucratic officials, few of whom were scholars.

The usual programme for our domestic conferences was for single-day meetings in Spring and late Autumn with a weekend conference in summer. At the day meetings there would be a broad theme such as siege warfare, civil-military relations or amphibious operations to be explored in four sessions covering different periods. Most members were chiefly interested in 20th century history, but it was important to give authorities on earlier periods a fair say, for example Ian Roy on the 17th century and Chris Duffy, a former Secretary-General, on the 18th. I would estimate that over all the meetings during my presidency the average would be one outstanding paper, two good ones and one sub-standard, but this may be a bit severe because some members were keen amateurs with limited experience or leisure for research. On the other hand some members were recognised authorities, such as Chris Duffy on Frederick the Great, who regularly addressed other history groups.

The weekend conferences offered much more scope to examine a specific theme, such as generalship in the First World War or the defeat of France in 1940. I recall a particularly lively discussion of invasion scares before 1914 and the 'future war fiction' associated with them. Combined operations in the Second World War was the subject of another successful meeting.

Most of our Spring meetings were held in Oxford, for about eight years at Rhodes House and then at Lady Margaret Hall where we had a vital contact in Dr Christine Gerrard, a lecturer in English Literature but also the wife of Duncan Anderson, Chandler's successor as head of department at Sandhurst. Another favourite weekend venue was the attractive campus of Buckingham University on the banks of the river Ouse. I recall the late General Sir Anthony Farrar-Hockley delivering a brilliant talk there without a note. On another occasion an extremely earnest Cambridge doctoral candidate gave an immensely detailed account of the Dieppe Raid. Since he had mentioned the high German consumption of beer a wag asked him if they received a discount on returned bottles. He replied that he was pretty sure they did, but more research was required before he could give a definite answer.

We held one conference in Chester but this proved a difficult 'away game' for London members working late on Fridays. Our host, with good intentions, had set up a grand reception for us with the mayor and other local worthies, but at the appointed time only three or four of us had arrived. The atmosphere was somewhat strained and we gallant few had to drink an awful lot of sherry.

At one of our weekend meetings at Bedford a mutiny was narrowly averted. I had arranged a full programme, including one session on the Friday evening, because the proceedings were intended to provide the basis for a book on the battle of France in 1940. At dinner a member (the same joker who had asked about the beer bottles) stood up and announced that the evening session was cancelled because it would interfere with plans to go to the local pub. I replied that we needed this session and the speaker (a major-general) was ready with his paper. If the pub visit took priority I would resign immediately and drive home. The lecture went ahead but the incident made plain what I had only suspected before; namely that for a small minority drinking time away from wives and family was a chief attraction for these meetings.

To round off the discussion of our one-day conferences, our secretaries managed to book a variety of attractive venues including: Rochester (my first in charge), Sandhurst, the Staff College, Bagshot Park (once the home of the Duke of Connaught), Bournemouth, Oakham, Dauntsey's school and the officers' messes at Tidworth and Shrivenham. I managed to arrange a meeting at Fawley Court near my home where the sessions were held in an elegant 18th century salon enhanced by wood carvings by Grinling Gibbons.

Probably our most popular venue, where we met on two occasions was the Guards officers' mess in Combermere barracks at Windsor, secured for us through the good offices of Simon Doughty, himself a Life Guards colonel. At one of these Michael Howard gave an outstanding talk on the special ethos of the Guards regiments, based on his own wartime experiences as a Coldstreamer. One point I particularly recall is the tradition that the officers should live as comfortably and elegantly as possible, even in the midst of battle.

It is not for me to evaluate my own contribution to the development of BCMH during my twenty years in office, but there had certainly been a transformation in nearly every aspect of our organisation: regular meetings and an audit at the A.G.M., a detailed list of members with addresses, battlefield tours, publications and a constitution. All this could not have happened without dedicated secretaries and committee members with the backing of a core of enthusiasts such as John and Celia Lee, Steve and Phylomena Badsey, Peter Robinson, Mike Hibberd, Laurie Milner and many others.

Although I had no hint of any 'Bond must go' agitations I felt it was right to resign after twenty years in case any members felt I was overstaying my welcome. I gave due notice of my intention to resign while searching for a successor who would maintain standards and perhaps improve on them. I thought an established academic would be preferable to set a personal example and attract top class visiting speakers. Unfortunately three of our distinguished members declined because they were too busy, but I was sure we had found a winner in Dr Richard Holmes because he combined an excellent publishing record with an outstanding reputation as a television presenter of campaigns and battles. Alas, he was already in poor health when he took over and died after only a few years in office, after a brave effort to keep going for as long as possible. I have deliberately distanced myself from BCMH since retiring and leave its later history to another hand.

8

Battlefield Tours

In the 1960s there was much less interest in exploring battlefields than there is today; many specialist companies now providing package tours even to distant war theatres such as the Crimea and South Africa. Books such as Martin Middlebrook's *The First Day on the Somme* (1975) surely inspired many young historians, and probably many more were influenced by the late Richard Holmes' brilliant television programmes.

No one ever suggested to me that a detailed knowledge of battlefields should form a part of my professional training, but when I decided to offer a new undergraduate special subject on 'Gallipoli' in place of Michael Howard's 'Franco-Prussian War' I considered it essential to see the terrain which had so critically affected every aspect of the operations and their tragic outcome. I believe I had already been influenced by John North's elegiac account *Gallipoli, the Fading Vision* (1936) and certainly by Robert Rhode James' *Gallipoli* (1965), so I had a strong mental image of the war theatre.

Accordingly, in September 1969, my wife and I travelled by rail and coach via Munich to Istanbul and then by boat to Eceabat, a small town on the European coast of the Dardanelles. I recall the small hotel as one of the worst I ever stayed in: there was a pervasive smell of rotten fish, and one pulled the lavatory chain at the risk of flooding.

There were no proper roads or dwellings in the battle area but we were fortunate to arrange lifts with the War Graves Commission, whose officials took us out in their truck early in the morning and collected us at an agreed place in late afternoon. We must have taken food and water but, alas, I seem to have made no notes. In dry, clement weather we walked for hours from the three principal landing areas of 1915: Cape Helles, Anzac Cove and Suvla

Bay. I do not remember meeting a single human being as we tramped the harsh terrain of scrub, sand and dried water courses. We had arrived just in time to see the battle area pretty much as it had been left after the First World War. Already rows of newly-planted conifers were beginning to obscure some trench lines and tracks, and I feel sure tourism has greatly altered the scene since then. There was still rusty debris to mark the dramatic landing at Cape Helles, plenty of cartridge cases and an occasional human skull in the undergrowth to remind us of the intense fighting in 1915, but otherwise there was just a formidable landscape in which no military planner would willingly have embarked on an attritional campaign. Lack of water greatly handicapped the Allied advance. What features stick in the mind after all these years? At Helles one could see at once that the Turkish machine gunners had the advantages of high ground fortification and good cover to wreak carnage on the unprotected soldiers as they landed. The famous cliffs were not so steep here as legend suggests because my wife could scale them, but more striking was the narrowness of the beaches, mere strips of sand a few yards deep on which to land all the men, animals, equipment and, not least important, medical facilities. At Anzac Cove the most striking feature was the constricted area for deployment dominated by almost sheer cliffs such as Walker's Ridge and Russell's Top. Suvla Bay provided much better access for landing but there the troops were faced with an expanse of arid salt flats hemmed in by a low ridge (Tekke Tepe) which gave the defenders an almost impenetrable line.

Our most memorable achievement was to scramble our way to the summit of Chunuk Bair from which the sparkle of the Narrows in the Dardanelles could just be seen. Years later I was irritated to hear a young lecturer criticise the slowness of the Right Assaulting Column's advance to the summit in the ill-fated attack on 6 August. It had taken me, a fit young man, several hours to force a way through the dense scrub and twisted water channels and arrive at the top exhausted; and no one was trying to kill me.

The great handicaps facing allied planners and commanders in this theatre in 1915 were starkly exposed by our brief visit. The bases for supply and reinforcements were far away; responsibility between the Army and Naval commanders was ambivalent and the former's headquarters had of necessity to be located on an offshore island; there was no natural harbour along the whole battle area so all the moorings and docking facilities had to be improvised and maintained against the elements. This list of intractable problems could be easily extended but the operational situation is clear. The courage of commanders and troops was unlikely to prevail against an entrenched enemy on higher ground, and with an easier supply line, unless strategic surprise could be achieved. Success seemed tantalisingly close on several occasions, including the naval assault on 18 March and the initial landings on 25 April, but eventually the impossibility of overcoming these handicaps against a stubborn opponent had to be accepted. In teaching this subject for a decade or more I was always aware of the great benefit I had derived from my brief visit to the peninsula.

I had read about the Somme campaign and given broad-brush lectures on it for several years before I visited the battlefields. I recall my surprise on first learning that on 1 July 1916 the British had advanced across and to the east of the Ancre, a mere tributary of the Somme which lay several miles behind the Allied front. I had a general notion of where the front line was located at the outset and knew the names of some of the famous villages involved, such as Thiepval, La Boisselle, Pozières, Fricourt and Montauban, but I had no grasp of the terrain and even less of the dramatic impact caused by so many war cemeteries crowded into such a small area.

I was extremely fortunate to make my first visit on a Martin Middlebrook tour. We were based at La Basilique in the centre of Albert and given a thorough grounding in the location of the front line from Gommecourt to Carnoy. Martin was immensely well-informed, an enthusiast and a good communicator. He held a sort of competition on the coach to help us remember what we had seen and, learning that I was an academic, subjected me to a particularly tough grilling. The prize was a fuse cap, much prized at the time. My wife, who accompanied me, felt that too much time was spent at cemeteries, and Martin did make additional diversions to please individuals who wanted to visit the graves of relatives. However I came to see, in time, that these landmarks were not only tragic memorials but also essential markers to specific actions and to the units engaged there. My only disappointment was that Martin concentrated so narrowly on the fateful first day that he could not spare time to take us to later episodes in the campaign. I particularly wanted to see Mametz Wood because I had long been a devotee of David Jones' epic poem *In Parenthesis*, and knew that other famous writers had fought there; Basil Liddell Hart being gassed in the wood and Robert Graves suffering such a serious wound that he was listed among the dead. This brief tour made a tremendous, positive impact so that I vowed to return as often as possible and get to explore the whole theatre of operations.

This I did from about 1990 onwards, usually making visits in Spring and Autumn. Most years I took my small MA Special Subject class, when possible at the beginning of term in early October to enthuse them for the course ahead. This seemed to work well, particularly in fostering a sense of group identity. One year we went in February, and I particularly recall our struggling through the dense undergrowth of the whole of Mametz Wood in the direction of the British advance. Soaked by torrential rain, a Job's comforter remarked 'all we need now is snow'. As we emerged onto the Bazentin road the snow began to fall. We gratefully found refuge in 'The Burma Star' café in Pozières where even the leathery steaks were eagerly consumed.

On these occasions we always stayed at La Basilique, developing such good relations with the owners that they entrusted us with the front door keys on Saturday evenings and Sunday mornings when they were away at (I think) Abbeville. Our two regular drivers were John Lee and Peter Robinson, both King's MAs in War Studies, the former becoming an eminent battlefield tour guide and the latter, a career policeman, later achieving a doctorate. There were inevitably a few mishaps such as a badly cut hand, losing keys and nearly running out of petrol in the desolate area around Ginchy, but there were far more memorable episodes, fostering friendships as well as introducing beginners to the importance of battlefield terrain.

My other regular visits occurred mostly in the Spring, with two friends, when we found a permanent and very comfortable base in a family guesthouse 'Les Galets' on the minor road between Auchonvillers and Beaumont Hamel. It was built, more recently of course, right on the start line of the attack towards the Redan on 1 July and within walking distance of Newfoundland Park and the Hawthorn crater. Even in poor weather these were delightful days, even allowing that distance in time tends to bestow a roseate tint. My particular friends, who did the driving, were Nigel Cave whose encyclopaedic knowledge of the battle could be daunting; Simon Doughty, already mentioned as a Guards officer and an MA in War Studies; and Tony Hampshire who obtained a doctorate under my supervision at the age of seventy after a career in business. Other friends who made the outing more than once included Colin Hook, Michael Piercy and Tom Ishizu, who had also taken the War Studies MA and would later invite me on several occasions to lecture in Japan.

We aimed to explore at least one new item on each visit whether a cemetery, remains of a trench, fortification, unit or personal memorial, or simply an unexplored track with a previously unseen vista. In addition to Nigel Cave's erudition there was available the truly comprehensive guidebook in Martin and Mary Middlebrook's *The Somme Battlefields* (1991) which set us challenges of places to visit that could never be fully achieved.

Historians should not have favourite battles but there are places in the Somme area that I shall always recall with affection. I treasure the wonderful picnic lunches we held at the tiny hilltop copse with one of the Caribou memorials just beyond Guedecourt, the furthest point reached by the Allies on the whole front in 1916. Another favourite place for lunch was the New Zealand Memorial on the crest of the ridge above Delville Wood with magnificent views to the south. But the views from our lodgings at 'Les Galets' took some beating: we could just see the trees marking the cemetery by the Hawthorn Crater; to the south lay the Redan and Beaumont Hamel; while to the west I could watch vehicles apparently plunge off the ridge as the road suddenly dipped towards Serre. After a hard day's walking, dinners at the auberge in Authuille followed by a drive back in the dark could be most happy occasions. It may seem macabre but many of the cemeteries had their own special appeal, including the Guards Cemetery at Lesboeufs, the steeply sloping cemetery at Authuille with its many Indian graves, and, to stray from the Somme towards Cambrai, the Tank Corps memorial at Louverval with stone carvings by Eric Gill on the entrance portico, and the laconic description of a lost lover – 'Netty's Chum'.

Our visits were not of course confined to the Somme area. There were the Arras offensives of 1915 and 1917 to explore with an opportunity to tour the remarkable tunnel system under the city, recently re-opened to the public.

Although the lie of the land and the intersecting canals make the Cambrai battlefield harder to follow, we often followed the main thrust of the Allied offensive through Flesquières to the Bourlon ridge. Though in private grounds fascinating German deep dugout shafts and signed emplacements could be viewed from Flesquières and, more recently, the publicly displayed tank renovated by a local man and housed in his barn.

Although I have visited other battle areas such as Third Ypres and the German offensive towards Hazebrouck in March–April 1918, I still feel a special emotional attraction to the Somme. This is partly due to the inspiration of Middlebrook's tour, but more importantly that the area remains largely unspoilt and beautiful, while the slowly unfolding campaign can be more easily followed by car and on foot. It saddens me that I may have paid my last visit to this enchanted ground.

I have visited numerous Second World War battlefields, or more accurately critical points, but only occasionally as the organiser or chief speaker. Following the German advance in May 1940 through the Ardennes to the river Meuse I was astonished by the speed of the advance and the comparative ease with which the leading infantry units crossed the river almost under the noses of the French defenders; their huge gun emplacements still much in evidence. But what struck me more forcibly, because so rarely open to the public, was a visit to the underground tunnels of a sector of the Maginot Line which was specially arranged for us (a group of Staff College officers) by a local preservation society. We travelled a mile or so on the open carriages of the miniature railway and were shown the remarkable facilities, kitchens, cinemas, medical quarters which had kept the garrison safe and comfortable during the months of the 'Phoney War'. The reasons behind this static defensive mentality were self-evident – to protect the soil of France with minimum losses – but it was still a dubious strategy in a new era of fast mechanised columns supported by powerful airforces.

Although I took part in several tours of the Normandy battle theatre I was essentially a spectator and, to my later regret, was never so fully engaged as at Gallipoli or the Somme. What stays vividly in the memory, however, are the hulks of the enormous artificial harbours looming through the early mists off the Arromanches beaches. From a teaching viewpoint it was important to see the celebrated bocage country west of Caen: the small fields with dense hedgerows and deep ditches certainly did present a formidable obstacle to the Allied advance, but the area involved, contrary to the assumption in many student essays, was not all-encompassing. Two other dramatic aspects of the campaign remain vivid in my memory. First, the brilliant capture by a single gliderborne company of 6th Airborne Division in the early hours of 6 June of the 'Pegasus Bridge' over the Orne Canal at Bénouville.

Secondly, the awesome spectacle from the surrounding heights of the final closure of the Falaise pocket:

> The Germans had suffered a grievous defeat. They lost somewhere between 25,000 and 50,000 men who were taken prisoner and another 5,000 to 10,000 killed. The terrain in the Falaise area held the charred

> and destroyed remains of German weapons, equipment and vehicles, and the bloated bodies of thousands of dead horses.
>
> (I.C.B. Dear and M.R.D. Foot *The Oxford Companion to the Second World War* p812)

The one episode in which I did play a leading role as both organiser and speaker involved the British 'counter-attack' around Arras on 21 May 1940. My lengthy research paper has recently been republished in my collection of essays *From Liddell Hart to Joan Littlewood* (Helion, 2015) so need not be discussed in much detail here. In the early 1980s I was a member of a small History Group which met in the former C.I.G.S's room in the Old War Office with the aim of discovering whether historical counter-strokes might yield lessons relevant to NATO in the event of a Soviet offensive in Western Europe. I chose this episode in the German advance to the Channel, already much debated, because I was familiar with the campaign as a result of several publications and close study in my undergraduate special subject class.

In addition to personal visits with friends I led group visits by a batch of officers from the Camberley Staff College; a Territorial Army brigade; and the British Commission for Military History, of which I was then President. The British force, nominally commanded by General Harold Franklyn, was very small, improvised at short notice, badly co-ordinated (between infantry, tanks and artillery) and with an ill-defined mission. It was, to say the least, risky, to talk of a 'mopping up' operation in face of the rapidly advancing 7th Panzer Division commanded by General Rommel.

Nevertheless the force, consisting essentially of two infantry and two tank battalions, advancing in two columns round the west of Arras, enjoyed astonishing success for a few hours which raised speculation at the time and ever since as to what 'might have been'. This ephemeral success was due to catching leading German units by surprise and unprepared to guard their flanks. Their artillery at first made little impression on the British tanks while infantry units were scattered: a unique and encouraging sight in this campaign. However, without air cover and with the artillery lagging behind, the two columns lost momentum in the late afternoon; the enemy then counter-attacked and by nightfall the remnants were driven back towards their starting point near Vimy. Later research would show that the Wehrmacht high command, including its chief of staff Franz Halder, were only briefly thrown into confusion. The immediate crisis was quickly rectified and the drive towards the Channel ports resumed.

This brief episode has retained its fascination for historians because it is now clear that Hitler and some of his most senior commanders, such as Field Marshal Von Rundstedt, expected a major Allied counter-attack and feared that their headlong rush towards the Channel coast would result in a disaster. A few days later Hitler peremptorily halted Guderian's Panzer Corps for two days thus allowing an important breathing space for the Allies to organise a defensive perimeter around Dunkirk. Other important factors were involved in the 'miraculous escape' by so many soldiers from the port and the beaches but the Panzers' pause certainly helped. If there was a lesson to be learnt which might be applicable in other circumstances the crucial missing elements in May 1940 were obvious. The counter-stroke forces had to be much larger (divisions rather than battalions); they had to be concentrated much earlier (several days rather than hours); air support was essential; the commander's objective had to be clearly-defined; and allied (i.e. French) co-operation was essential. Since these conditions were completely lacking in the desperate retreat of the British Field Force any success could only be short-lived and tactical, not strategic.

I hope these 'lessons' were absorbed by the officers and students in the tours I conducted. In practice it was difficult to follow the advances of the separate columns, and the westward spread of Arras and its suburbs with industrial developments south of the city have created further obstacles. Nevertheless this operation has frequently been the subject of Staff Rides and other touring parties. Although I remain sceptical about the historical lessons to be learnt from these events I still believe that theoretical discussion can be useful provided it is based on a really thorough examination of the evidence.

Though not strictly a battlefield tour I will conclude this section with a brief account of my visit to Calais to commemorate the heroic defence of the town by C.N. Nicholson's brigade against 10th Panzer Division in May 1940. *The Times* newspaper sponsored a one day cruise on which I was to be the lecturer and was to suggest some V.I.Ps to add distinction to the venture. The outing was so well subscribed that I had to deliver the same lecture twice. One of the distinguished guests, General Sir Anthony Farrar-Hockley chaired my first lecture and when he heard that it had to be repeated insisted on chairing the second as well, thus forfeiting his lunch. This is the kind of unselfish generosity that one never forgets. I also managed to kiss the other famous V.I.P, Dame

Vera Lynn, but I regret to report that she did not sing. The party was given a tour of Calais with a meeting at the town hall and a closing ceremony at the memorial on the quay. The purpose of my lecture was to contend that the brigade's stubborn resistance against overwhelming odds until the afternoon of 26 May was a key factor in enabling the evacuation of the great majority of the British Field Force. I thought then, and still do, that Hitler's 'halt order' to the Panzer advance between 24 and 26 May was even more important, but the official history (L.F. Ellis *The War in France and Flanders 1939–1940*) makes a strong case that 30th Brigade's resistance did permit Dunkirk's western perimeter to be strengthened. What is beyond dispute is that the War Office was prepared to allow the remnant of the garrison to be evacuated but acceded to the local French commander's insistence that they fight to the last man – a dubious contribution to the spirit of allied unity.

In general I now think that battlefield tours, with clear objectives and expert lecturers, are an essential part of the military historian's training. I only wish I had started earlier and explored more campaigns on the ground.

9

Bad Days at the Office

Perhaps there was a golden age when Oxbridge dons (nearly all bachelors) had very little obligatory teaching and had ample leisure to drink sherry and attempt to undermine their rivals' reputations. If this Utopia had ever existed it had largely vanished during the Second World War. Could *Zuleika Dobson* (1911) have been recreated in post-1945 Oxford? Many hitherto sheltered dons saw active service, while less active ones did their bit for the war effort at home, for example, as did Edmund Blunden, by teaching map-reading to officer cadets. Returning veterans were eager for serious study and expected professional dedication from their tutors. Most had to think about earning a living after three or four fleeting years. In addition there was a new influx of grammar school pupils, like myself, who had no money at all behind them, no social connections and no rich uncle to bail them out if they failed. Of course there were exceptions to all these generalisations. There were, for example, still a few incompetent dons who were appalling lecturers, did the minimum of tutorial teaching and published nothing.

King's College, London had a conservative, even stuffy, reputation while its location in Central London lacked the glamour of 'dreaming spires'. There were residential halls in the suburbs, but most students and their teachers had to commute from quite a distance. This greatly inhibited social life in the evenings and some colleagues, unlike me, never even took a proper lunch break. Some teachers were of course more energetic and conscientious than others, but there was little scope for idleness. It was a full and often hectic life of lectures, seminars, staff meetings, with a plethora of College and University committees.

This introduction must not in any way be regarded as a complaint or criticism: it was a way of life I had striven to enter and I was determined to make the most of it. What I do want to suggest is that in thirty-five years of teaching and holding responsible positions concerned with such matters as entrance interviews, examinations and staff appointments there were bound to be 'bad days at the office'. Mercifully I can remember only a few; merely fleeting shadows now but painful and distressing at the time.

For seventeen years War Studies lecturers endured narrow hutch-like cubicles on the third floor of the new, utilitarian Strand Building. On one occasion a would-be research student whom Mike Dockrill and I had interviewed told us he would reject an offer anyway. Just think of it, he said, even if I succeeded I could finish up like you two. This was unfair but still painful; we needed modest rooms but still spacious enough to hold a small class. This I did not enjoy between 1971 and 1987.

A completely different kind of embarrassment arose over the annual War Studies Lecture for which I was responsible as Chairman of the Board for several years. The name of Martin Gilbert was proposed as the recently appointed biographer of Sir Winston Churchill. Could we not get in early and ask him to give us an insight into his subject's stormy career in the 1920s and 1930s before publication? One or at most two lectures was the norm but Professor D.C. Watt insisted that so great a national figure must have four.

Gilbert accepted and it was my duty to chair for him. The first lecture was a disaster: he had no script, only a bundle of notes which he shuffled nervously. There was no attempt to paint a broad picture; indeed no clear argument at all, just one damn thing after another. Bewailing my fate before the second lecture I remarked to Mike Dockrill through an open door that I dreaded the approaching ordeal. Martin was standing within touching distance and must have heard every word; a moment when one wishes the earth would open up. The really bitter denouement came with the post mortem at the next Board meeting when D.C. Watt calmly remarked 'Of course everyone knows that Gilbert is a lousy lecturer.' Two further points must be added: Martin helped me on several occasions, especially over maps, and he did improve a lot as a speaker in his later years.

As the person responsible for admitting and monitoring the progress of the M.Phil–PhD candidates over may years I had numerous difficulties with students who did not keep in regular touch with their supervisors; took far too long (i.e. more than five or six years) to present their theses; and worst of all, gave up without telling anyone. One candidate, who had been passed on to me by a colleague because he could not decide on a topic, never so far as I remember, communicated with me at all. Since his father was then head of an Oxbridge college he was hardly impoverished or an outsider who did not know the rules. Indeed he was in receipt of a research grant so his success was important to the department. I wrote him a stern letter asking him to clarify his intentions, only to receive a very angry phone call from his mother, accusing us of failing to give her son proper supervision. He had already abandoned research, she told me, and had found a job. Many years later I saw him once or twice on Antiques Roadshow as an expert, I think, on furniture. At the time of his withdrawal a polite, truthful reply would have been appreciated.

Up to a point I understood the dilemma of research students who had given up, for good and not so good reasons, but found it difficult to admit their failure, but their lack of co-operation caused me countless 'bad days'. At the termly inquisition into 'progress' I did my best to make a case for them, but as the years rolled by colleagues would ever more impatiently ask for their expected completion date. In some cases I had to respond wearily 'don't know'. One or two newcomers thought I was too lax and they would soon be able to sort things out. 'Summon them for interview and demand an answer' was their solution, but in the really hard cases, they had to admit failure. My solution was to terminate their link with the department after due time and ample warnings, but this was not generally approved. Perhaps university regulations were not sufficiently clear about the maximum period allowed. The situation became worse in my final years so that I imagined my tormentors leaning over my death bed to demand 'when are Mr X and Mr Y going to submit?' Fortunately retirement came to my rescue before death.

Careless talk costs jobs, or may at least put them at risk. As chairman of the MA Examination Board I knew that one must never, never discuss results with candidates before these were made public, and even then extreme caution is recommended. I once made an accidental slip in this regard which I at once regretted. I had just marked a batch of papers in which an American student had done badly. Scripts were numbered but as chairman I must have had the key to names. Meeting her by chance in the corridor she volunteered the information that she planned to go for a higher degree at another centre of learning. Thinking I might moderate the shock if she failed, I merely advised her to await the results before she made a final decision. She at once assumed that I already knew she had failed. She told me she had a lawyer boyfriend in Brussels who would initiate legal action against me, though it was not clear what the charge would be. It was a 'bad day' for me but I did not worry unduly since I had not given her any definite information. As it turned out she secured an overall pass and no more was said. The incident re-inforced what I already knew: never say anything to an exam candidate about results even if you are trying to be kind or comforting. Well-intentioned words or gestures are almost certain to be misunderstood or resented.

A different case of an MA candidate who had failed caused me much more trouble than a mere 'bad day'. This man was an Asian and probably a serving officer, who went to two of my colleagues and told them he could not go home because he would be disgraced. To save his honour could they arrange a special re-sit for him in September (this was July or early August) when he would surely pass? In sympathy they told him this could be done. They cleared this decision with the head of department and only then came to me, as chairman of the examiners, to set a re-sit date and have new papers prepared. I had just written to the other failures telling them they would have another chance next summer and I could not see how we could arrange an early exam for this 'special case'. I spent a couple of sleepless nights going over and over this matter before writing to the University Board of Examiners for a ruling. The reply was clear: regulations only permitted an early re-sit if the candidate had missed all or part of the exams through illness which would have to be medically certified. I wrote briefly to my colleagues saying that their mistake, however well-intentioned, had caused me a great deal of anxiety. The single word 'sorry' would have sufficed to settle the matter but neither colleague ever issued it. I do not know if the individual concerned passed at the second attempt.

My last example of a 'bad day' caused by exam failure at MA level concerns a young Nigerian woman. When she entered my room she was in such a rage that her features looked pale. If she had possessed a knife I feel sure she would have stabbed me. She said she had never failed an exam before and could not believe she had done so now. I managed to calm her down and read out a few extracts from her answers which I had on the table, suggesting that her emotional tirades were expressing her feelings but not answering the question. What was required was cool reasoning in plain English, which, I reassured her, must have been evident in her class essays or she would not have been given good grades. To my relief she completely accepted my judgment and asked if I would read some practice essays before she re-took the exam. Of course I agreed and was able to give her good marks for the four or five essays she handed in, including at least one on Clausewitz, who was a safe banker for an exam question. No one before or since had ever worked so hard to improve their essay presentation. I was delighted that she passed the re-sit comfortably but also glad that she was unarmed at our first meeting.

From its beginning in 1965 the MA class had been international in composition. Even in the early years when the total annual intake was about twenty I recall that New Zealand, Canada, the United States, Israel, Nigeria and Japan were represented, and after I had visited Pakistan in 1968 there was always at least one Pakistani officer present. Inevitably there were a few failures but, contrary to rumours, there was never a quota. One year, however, there appeared to be a serious problem when all the European or 'Western' candidates passed whereas all the African and Asian candidates failed. This was an unfortunate co-incidence but awkward questions were asked by senior College officials. If the figures appeared in the press there would be accusations of racial prejudice and demands that 'heads should roll', mine being high on the list. Our conscience was clear because all the exam scripts were identified by numbers rather than names so that the markers would not know the names. There was of course the additional safeguard that the external examiner would know none of the candidates.

Nevertheless there was a real underlying problem though it was essentially cultural and certainly not racial. Wherever possible we (Wolf Mendl and myself for many years) gave potential candidates a stiff interview not only on their mental ability, (an upper second at BA level or its equivalent), but also their command of written English. Students from English-speaking countries would usually have had experience in writing essays but even some of them would struggle under the pressure of three hour exam papers. Students from other countries with no experience of the British system and uncertain skill in writing English might just about cope with the coursework, perhaps with a bit of help, but would sometimes be defeated by the requirement to write three answers in three hours on very searching questions. An oral examination for borderline candidates would have helped, but was considered too time-consuming to implement. A more practical solution was to give coursework grades a place in the final result, as of course was always the case with mini-theses or extended essays. This has certainly been tried and is probably used much more widely now than in my time. The main drawbacks lay in ensuring that the work was entirely that of the candidate; in obtaining internal and external validation; and in preventing crafty students specialising in one area of study. Sometimes, by judicious choice of exam questions students could obtain their MA degree more narrowly in 'Air Power' or 'Sea Power' rather than 'War Studies' proper.

I must admit, in concluding the topic, that there was unavoidable tension between admitting large numbers of qualified students, maintaining high standards and ensuring that as few as possible failed. I believe that on the whole we succeeded on the last point: with careful advice on why a candidate had failed and what they must do to improve, the second opportunity usually allowed genuine borderline cases to pass. As chairman of the MA Exam Board I always tried to persuade my colleagues to err on the side of generosity, rather than ruthless number-crunching, in marginal cases where the candidate had clearly tried hard under difficult circumstances, such as holding down a demanding job or working without access to important sources for revision.

My long stint as chairman of the MA Board ended in confusion and recriminations: a shocking surprise to me as more than twenty years had passed without any serious upset. The basic problem was that three or four of our lecturers had been excused attendance at the final meeting to attend a conference in Split. Some of them had not finalised their marks internally or with the external examiner, an Oxford notable who did nothing to solve the issue. To compound the difficulty, our then secretary was in an uncooperative mood and took a relaxed attitude to completing the mark sheet.

The embarrassing result can be imagined. As the individual marks were read out gaps began to appear and it became clear that in many cases a final result could not be obtained. The meeting had to be abandoned: a unique and shameful episode. Professor Freedman was understandably angry and, for the only time ever, raged at me for making the Department a laughing-stock. From my viewpoint this was a classic instance of responsibility without power. I had not given the absentees permission to miss the meeting and I had had to rely on their good will and cooperation to complete and hand in their marks before leaving. I had tried hard to persuade the secretary to chase up the missing marks and fill in the columns but she had not done so. I would not have lacked the courage to take punitive measures against errant colleagues but there was nothing I could do. What I could do of course was to resign. I do not recall any formal notice to this effect, but after the fiasco just described it was surely inevitable. I cannot say I regretted the removal of this annual chore for one moment.

My last 'bad day at the office' was a scarcely credible episode which dogged me for several years. In my responsibility for admitting research students I had approved the entry of an Israeli who seemed to be suitably qualified. A relevant background influence on me was that the Department was in favour of boosting research numbers, and that Israelis were highly regarded as generally clever, hard working and anxious to succeed. This student's main sponsor provided only a brief positive reference, but the other, Dr Uri Bialer was not only a proven scholar but also a friend. I found a colleague, Dr Philip Sabin, who was willing to supervise the Israeli's project and we both signed or initialled a sheet of paper approving the application. So far so good, but the sheet of paper was never typed up and remained in its rough state to haunt me. Whether the candidate did any work for Dr Sabin I don't know, but he became disillusioned with research, with King's College, by implication with me and with everyone except himself. The really unusual aspect of this case was that he decided to sue the College for wrongful admission, claiming that his Israeli grades were not good enough for doctoral research and this should have been spotted. This seemed to me an incredible line to take: his referees had supported him and he had achieved his goal of coming to King's College, London to do doctoral research.

This matter should not have gone any further, but the College was naturally opposed to paying damages (or risk the case causing adverse publicity), and was determined to defend its record in court. The College solicitor rang me and asked if I had signed the scrap of paper referred to earlier. I had done so and consequently must be ready to appear in court as a defence witness. What was really infuriating was that this procedure was repeated for several years, invariably with a different solicitor and the same incredulous question – had I signed this scrap of paper? This telephone call usually occurred in late summer so that if I had heeded the instruction to stand by for a court summons I would have missed overseas conferences already arranged. I ignored these instructions on the assumption that the claimant's case was ludicrous and that he was bluffing. So far as I know my hunch was correct: the case did not go to court and the College did not pay damages. I am still puzzled, however, by the psychology behind this very strange case, and relieved that I did not suffer further for my minor errors in not ensuring that the admission form was fully written up, properly signed by both academics, and filed.

10

Bad Days in the Lecture Hall

All public speakers will have experienced episodes they would prefer to forget: getting lost, forgetting notes, wrong dates, misleading briefings or just performing badly. In the hope that a few of my 'bad days' may be illuminating or amusing I will offer a selection.

Talking to school classes can be particularly hazardous. What is the age group and how well-informed are they? Will there be a disturbing procession of groups shuffling out to prep or other classes?

At Ampleforth College I had barely begun a lecture on the First World War when a small boy stood up and asked 'what do you mean by macabre?' I had scarcely answered that when he again interrupted by saying that my remarks about British shell production in 1914 being based on expenditures in the South African War were nonsense, and he then walked out without waiting for my explanation. Afterwards I was told that he had earlier suffered a nervous breakdown and had only just returned to school. Apparently my lecture had again tipped him over the edge.

I had previously given several successful talks at Stonyhurst College to a group of senior boys ('The History Bench') but on the last visit, when my topic was 'Fresh thinking on the First World War', I was confronting a younger group who had done no reading or thinking at all. 'What was Gallipoli?' was the first question which demonstrated I was in the wrong place. Young age groups could be quite challenging and stimulating provided they had been properly briefed and done some reading. A junior class at Eton gave me a testing time on 'Appeasement'; while at another school a very small boy asked me whether Jackie Fisher's reforms were a good thing or a bad thing for the Royal Navy.

At Stonyhurst I have given several enjoyable talks to the 'Senior Essay Society' composed of teachers and a variety of local people interested in history. At my last visit I enraged a middle aged woman by references to British soldiers executed during the First World War. She had every right to believe that this was a mistaken, even a wicked, policy, but was clearly riled by my refusal to condemn it utterly. She would not listen when I tried to explain the complex circumstances, including the fact that the great majority of those condemned to death had their sentences commuted, and also that it was now generally agreed that there had been some unjust convictions of individuals who in retrospect were recognised as severe cases of shell-shock. None of this appeased my antagonist so eventually I could only protest that I had not shot any of them myself. Quite recently I had another disappointing visit to speak to a history group at Harrow School. My wife and I came by car and were told to park at the bottom of the very steep hill on which the school is perched. We were both exhausted by the climb, but when I asked for a glass of water the senior boy who went to get it said that none was available. I had to insist that I would not start without it. I quickly found that the audience was mixed in age with few senior history students, little interest in what I had to say in comparing Britain's role in the two world wars, and no questions to raise. This was pretty much a waste of time because insufficient thought had been given to the arrangements; all too casual for an elderly professor at London University coming some distance by car.

When 'bad days' occur in lectures to undergraduate or adult groups they can be more upsetting because one assumes that the organisers have chosen the speaker and are well-aware of his or her special field of interest. Some time ago I addressed a local history group at nearby Beaconsfield on the Third Ypres or Passchendaele campaign of 1917. I was then more critical of British generalship and the course of operations than I am now, but had not counted on two members of the audience being fervent supporters of Haig and the campaign; could they even have been veterans? They gave me a hard time but I found consolation in the prospect of the splendid tea laid out in the vestibule as we came in. Our hopes were dashed: the tea was destined for a Women's Institute or similar meeting held in another room. It was a matter of 'goodbye and don't trouble us again'.

Just a few years ago I gave a generally well-received lecture on the First World War at a packed town hall in Sherborne. Again it was a lady who was provoked by my quoting Edmund Blunden's lines:

Why slept not I in Flanders clay
With all the murdered men?

She launched a harangue on the phrase 'murdered men' as demonstrating that Blunden had rightly condemned British strategy and operations as criminal policy against our own troops in a wicked war. I tried to argue that the poet could equally have meant that it was the enemy who had murdered our troops, and furthermore, it was clear from the context of my essay (in *Survivors of a Kind*) that what perturbed him most deeply was his own chance survival when so many worthier men had died. I was not able to convince her and left the meeting feeling that I had lost a peripheral argument that had diverted attention from my main themes.

At a lecture on 'Appeasement' at Aberystwyth University I encountered a dissenter who really did 'go for the jugular' in contesting my arguments, which were strongly critical of Neville Chamberlain and his policy. As soon as I stopped speaking a senior history lecturer at the University stood up and said that 'he disagreed with every word I had said'. This seemed to me a bit hard on words like 'the' and 'but', and even '1938' and 'Munich' might have escaped censure. This is a highly emotive subject, like fox-hunting, but it should be capable of rational discussion at a university. At last, after my critic had held forth for some time, I said that he evidently thought he should be giving the lecture, but since I had been invited and had travelled a long way, he should now let other members of the audience put questions to me. This met with a round of applause, suggesting to me that my critic's propensities for hogging the limelight were well-known.

At a large international conference at Péronne to open the Historial there in the early 1990s, I read a paper on how the battle of the Somme had been treated in British historiography. The paper was not based on deep research but it seemed at least adequate for the occasion and was later published. However there was present a young lecturer from Oxford who had written his doctorial thesis on a related subject. He told the audience that my paper was full of errors but he would confine himself to list just eight (or was it ten?) of them. This he proceeded to do at some length. Even if he was right in every detail this was bad practice. If a paper is really bad you can let the speaker know your opinion briefly and politely without trying to demolish it sentence by sentence.

I was present at a really embarrassing example where the speaker (an American) thought that Operation 'Overlord' had taken place in 1943, so that everything he said was a year out. This was in Caen of all places where the Allied invasion had destroyed the city in 1944 but no one at the conference said a word.

After a talk I gave to Niall Ferguson's class at Jesus College, Oxford a female student asked me bluntly why had I wasted my life studying war? I replied that if one wanted to teach history then war was the most exciting and dramatic aspect, but I doubt if this was persuasive. I could just as truthfully have replied that it was because I knew I was not good enough to earn a living by playing football or cricket.

On numerous occasions I believe that I have had a 'bad day' because I have not been properly briefed in advance or have misjudged the audience. Sometimes, as already mentioned, I have overestimated the audience's knowledge, but to err in the other direction can be very embarrassing. In my only visit to Copenhagen I was asked to address a group of officers studying British military policy in 1930s. I regarded myself as something of an expert, but discovered that they had been exploring particular issues in depth and had specific questions about documentary sources which I had either not read or forgotten. I have seldom felt so inadequate but believe I should have been better briefed about their course. A comparable case occurred with a WFA meeting where most audiences contain only a few well-read or expert members, but on a quite recent occasion I spoke to a group of about a dozen, four or so of whom already had doctorates while several were working towards a PhD or MPhil, all on aspects of my subject on the First World War. With advanced warning I would have presented a paper on which I had done more research, but as it was I felt I had disappointed them. On two occasions, in Suffolk and London, I also felt I had failed my audience when speaking, by request, about the Victorian Army: thereby 'meeting my Waterloo' as my wife kindly told me afterwards. A lifetime ago I had done extensive research on aspects of the Army c. 1860–1900, including reforms and campaigns, but I was rusty and didn't know what the audience expected. In retrospect I felt I had put too much emphasis on Cardwell's administrative reforms and not enough on colonial campaigns for the Suffolk group, while the London group expected me to concentrate on the South African War. Of course there may have been a few individuals who enjoyed both talks but you are lucky if you get complimented at the time. I have certainly not been given a chance to redeem myself with the London group whose headquarters is Buckingham University.

Much more embarrassing, even demoralising, was a talk I was asked to give to a group of Army officers at the end of their course held in a Bournemouth hotel. I should have been alerted by the words 'after dinner', but the organiser assured me that a serious academic topic was required. I opted for something on the lines of 'Is Clausewitz still relevant?', but it might just as well have been 'Is Bond still relevant?'. The dinner started late and went on and on. When I eventually stood up to speak coaches were already waiting to take officers back to Sandhurst. I was tired and irritable and spoke badly. Two or three members of the audience, including a former doctoral student of mine, criticised me sharply which rubbed salt into the wounds. I did eventually receive a cheque but it did not fully compensate for this fiasco. At any time before about 7.0pm this talk would have been at least adequate and my mindset positive; at 10.0pm it was just a bad joke.

I will end this rather gloomy section on a more positive note. In the early 1970s I made several visits to the USA, primarily to lecture at the Naval War College at Newport, Rhode Island, but there were opportunities to speak elsewhere. I made visits to the delightful campuses at Chapel Hill and Duke University in North Carolina. At the latter I was the guest of Theodore (Ted) Ropp, who I have mentioned earlier, a distinguished military historian, noted for his book *War in the Modern World*, but also an eccentric. He invited me to attend his research seminar, convening at 8.30am and containing some very bright soldiers and scholars. We sat around the table for several minutes before I asked who was to speak. 'You are,' Ropp replied and when asked the topic, 'you decide'. I was planning a book on Liddell Hart so was able to speak quite confidently about his ideas and reputation. I learnt later that Ropp did this deliberately because he believed an improvised talk would result in a more lively presentation and a better discussion, but it was a risky strategy. With a nervous or tired speaker it could be a disaster, but perhaps Ropp knew that I could cope and was, in effect, giving me a vote of confidence.

How does a chairman stop speakers who greatly overrun their allotted time? I love the story of the Oxford don who, bored to death by a colleague droning on, asked to be knocked unconscious to provide a respite. As he slumped under the table he was heard to plead 'Hit me again, I can still hear him'.

Anyone who has chaired academic proceedings will have experienced this dilemma: how do I stop the speaker without being rude or offending those who want to hear him or her to the end? At the American School in Paris at a conference to mark the fiftieth anniversary of the outbreak of the Second World War, I was asked to chair the last session of the afternoon with three speakers. Unfortunately there were late comers to be fitted in so two speakers were added to my panel. This was difficult enough but one of these, the last speaker of the session was a very distinguished Parisian female professor who took the stand with a thick sheaf of typescript which she was determined to read. As the closing time approached I did all I could, in the form of passing notes and frantic waving but she ignored me. Eventually the organiser, whose name I remember was Dr Pike, came raging up to the platform and berated me for ruining the conference. The translators were threatening to strike if the session was not stopped immediately. I suppose the lady was persuaded to stop eventually, but I could only have achieved this by rugby tackling her off the stage – a horrible image.

At least twice as chairman I risked the wrath of the audience by summarily stopping interventions from the floor. In Edinburgh there was a professor of French History whose habit was to ask the first question which was deliberately marginal or even unrelated to the paper given. I had witnessed this tactic severely upset a speaker and when it was tried in my session I immediately ruled him out of order. At an international conference in Prague I similarly stopped a very distinguished French professor who tried to prolong a tedious session after the bell had sounded for lunch. I don't regret these actions because I felt they were taken in the interests of the other speakers and the audience.

A very difficult crisis arose at an international conference in Middleburg in 1994 to commemorate the liberation of the Netherlands fifty years earlier. I chaired a session where all the speakers were veterans of the campaign. An American professor, A.J. Bacevich made a fiery intervention to denounce military historians for their incompetence, in particular for failing to throw light on the topics on the programme. The timing of this outburst seemed to me outrageous in a session of veteran speakers who had risked their lives to liberate the Netherlands, and I said so quite vehemently from the chair. A very unpleasant contretemps ensued which divided the audience, the organisers mostly siding with me. There was no reconciliation and no apology on either side; the rest of the conference took place in a very strained atmosphere.

My last example was a very unpleasant affair at a day conference I had arranged in the great hall at King's College on the subject of Operation

Overlord and the battle for Normandy. I heard that one of the speakers had written a personal account of a platoon's experience in the campaign, which was very popular, and was a recommended text at Sandhurst. Anxious that the speaker might feel constricted by the customary format of three papers in the hour to allow time for discussion, I invited him to lunch well in advance to make sure he understood and accepted this time limit. Despite my best efforts he went on well over his allotted time so that either the next speaker (Mike Dockrill) had to forfeit his talk or the discussion period discarded. This made me very angry and I told him so when writing to him afterwards. He then wrote a letter of complaint about me to the head of department who seemed to think I should apologise for possibly harming the College's reputation. There was no way I would do this, having taken such trouble to ensure that the proceedings would run smoothly.

As a postscript on a different aspect of chairmanship I recount, to my embarrassment, my experience at the research office in Freiburg (im Breisgau). I had attended several conferences there, always being allowed to speak in English to officers who were all fluent in the language. On my last visit (I think) I heard a distinguished American scholar read his paper in execrable German and was told, entirely reasonably, that as chairman my session would be conducted entirely in the home language. I could just about understand the questions, but my German was nowhere near fluent enough to permit me to conduct the discussion in that language. Somehow, with help from merciful friends, I got through the session but it was an ordeal I shall never forget, or repeat.

I have examined these examples and case studies mainly from my own viewpoint, but as an experienced organiser of seminars, lectures and conferences I am well aware of the difficulties of secretaries and committees facing so many uncertainties: speakers, venues, logistics and time tables. Sometimes those who do the organising opt for speakers and topics which interest them. I have twice recently lectured to WFA audiences on 'Eden and Macmillan' as memoir writers in the First World War clearly favoured by the secretary and perhaps the committee, whereas the audience only seemed interested in their later careers. At another WFA meeting someone must have opted for Siegfried Sassoon as my topic to address, but the only question I remember was what did he do in the Second World War, to which it would hardly be frivolous to reply: he played cricket on his estate in Wiltshire.

At the risk of concluding this section on a banal note I will list a few of the lessons I have learnt over a lifetime of lecturing and chairing. Do have a few notes just in case you are unwell. Don't try to cover too much ground: a few strong points will make more impact. Speak up but not too fast. An opening joke or amusing story will ease tension. Don't go on for too long: a weak paper will be excused if brief but waffling will cause animosity. Take questions seriously and try to draw in less confident people if there is a lull. Don't let yourself be irritated or distracted by hostile or silly questions, but don't allow yourself to be bullied either. Don't worry if listeners do not raise the questions you expect or hope for but tell them in advance the one thing they *will* remember, usually funny or outrageous. Above all if you are accompanied by a wife or partner listen to them and heed their advice.

11

Foreign Fields

1 – Pakistan, 1968

Early in 1968 Michael Howard was invited to visit Pakistan to offer advice on the drastic re-organisation of the military history programme at their equivalent of Sandhurst, the Pakistan Military Academy at Kakul near Abbotabad. This was part of the projected reform of the whole syllabus with the objective of granting BA degrees after two years of study. Michael was too busy to accept and passed the opportunity to me. I duly spent an interesting and eventful month in that country.

Although there were periods of leisure and outings to schools, military establishments and the surrounding countryside, it was a somewhat frantic and tiring experience, not least because day time temperatures were usually in the 90°s and in Lahore well over 100°. I spent the greater part of the time at the Pakistan Military Academy, Kakul; in the news more recently because Osama Bin Laden was discovered in hiding near the entrance and killed there. I was housed in a small hut where a servant brought me water and generally looked after me, it was rather primitive but acceptable. For the most part I was treated as a VIP though this was not so obvious when I later visited Quetta. I sat in on lectures and classes, interviewed civilian and military instructors and drew up an elaborate military history syllabus with a full list of recommended reading. This was discussed, with only minor reservations, both at Kakul and at the Army's headquarters in Rawalpindi. In retrospect I am surprised at the amount of work I put in and the self-confidence I displayed in dealing with senior officers, including the Commander-in-Chief and the Chief of Staff. In preparing this brief account I was delighted to re-discover my diary, written in a school exercise book, which I had not looked at for nearly fifty years. I hope the following notes and extracts will convey a more vivid impression than an account based on what I remember now.

On 30 August I landed at Rawalpindi airport in the early morning with the temperature around 90°. I was introduced to the British Council official because my visit was partly sponsored by that body. I was then driven up the Grand Trunk Road about 75 miles to Abbotabad (reminiscent of Aldershot but in the lee of the mountains) and on up the steep climb to Kakul. The evidence of extreme poverty made a shocking impact on me: squalid mud villages in a parched landscape, primitive ploughs, roads packed with people, old men staggering under fantastic loads.

31 August. I first met Brigadier A.O. Mitha, Commandant at Kakul and chief proponent of a radical modernisation of the P.M.A. He was the 'star' of this episode in my life. He was a very handsome, charismatic personality with advanced ideas on the need for a much better educated Pakistan Army. 'A lucid mind and very well-read, quoting *War and Peace* among other classics.' He hinted that he'd got me to come out to lend independent backing to his reforming plans. G.HQ was quite keen, but the majority of regimental officers needed to be converted.

I soon got to know and make friends with my chief assistant and companion, Major Mohammed Akram. He had recently obtained an MA in English Literature, comprising eight papers ranging from Chaucer to T.S. Eliot. He shared my love of Wordsworth but could not imagine what 'a host of golden daffodils' would look like in the Himalayan foothills. He took me to see the town of Abbotabad and particularly to visit the officers' mess and club of the famous First Frontier Force Regiment (The 'Piffers'). There was a strange archaic atmosphere in the Club and its library as though the clock had stopped in about 1935.

2 September. Major Akram took me on a tour of nearby military quarters, and to see a drill parade and riding school. Between 7pm and 12.45am Brigadier Mitha gave seven of us a delightful evening in the mess where he talked very freely. He said that after the war (1945) he had deliberately spent nine months alone to test himself. He had had an Austrian mistress for seven years who said she would leave him the day she felt satisfied. That day had clearly been reached some time ago. He drank about six whiskies and simply marched out to signal that the evening was over.

3 September. Akram took me to watch a battalion at PT exercises and training, and on to Burn Hall School where we had tea with the Head, Father Scanlon. It may seem bizarre to record that in periods of leisure I played snooker (badly), swam in a rather grubby pool and read *Kilvert's Diary* among other books.

4 September. Sat in on lectures where the blatant Muslim bias irritated me, particularly over the 'Amritsar Massacre' on which I had published an article disputing the received wisdom placing all the blame on the Raj. At least the Director of Studies, Dr Abbasi, mentioned the pro-Indian lobby in Britain from John Bright to the Webbs.

6 September. Taken on a full day tour by English friends along the Murree Road to Ayubia. There were wonderful views but the summit of Nanga Parbat was hidden by mist and cloud. The ski lift was closed so we continued to Murree. Then, as now, obsessed by animals, I gave most of my sandwiches to three hungry puppies.

7 September. Wrote up my military history scheme and made notes for my lecture on Clausewitz. Another memorable evening alone with Brig Mitha and his wife which again lasted until after midnight. He spoke, among many topics, of his fondness for English democracy and his dislike of the United States, particularly the discipline and assessment methods at West Point. The ideals of leisure and conversation fascinated him. How glad he was that I had come out, presumably because I was a sympathetic listener who shared his love of reading and serious discussion. He had had a stormy career and had faced three courts martial. His first experience of war was in the ferocious battle at Kohima in 1944. He played me some Indian music but also discussed Sibelius and other classical composers. On a later occasion he told me he was from Bombay but felt a stronger sense of identity with Pakistan through having to make the choice at partition in 1947. He was in sympathy with young people in revolt against authority. He was very critical of Pakistan's educational attitudes: there was no room for the real scholar or original thinker. His firm belief was that the Army was the only rock of order in Pakistan and would remain so for many years. He has proved to be right.

At the earlier meeting on 7 September, under a brilliant starry sky like nothing I had seen in Europe, Mitha courteously strolled to the gate with me – about one hundred yards – wearing a loose white native robe. He was very relaxed and friendly and it struck me that he showed off much less than when in front of his officers.

Meanwhile on 8 September Major Akram, with a driver, took me on a long tour to Tarbella via Haripur. There were beautiful mountain vistas but the largely dried-up river Indus was a disappointment. At Hassanabad we visited the Cadet College, one of the most important public schools in the country and closely resembling the English model, including cricket. I suffered severely from the heat on these journeys, drinking 'Seven Up' and other fizzy liquids when possible.

10 September. Wrote up the revised syllabus in my room and then discussed it with Akram and the senior civilian teachers, whose attitude to their work seemed to me peevish and negative. Akram also hinted that Mitha's open-mindedness had its limits. The former had vainly challenged Mitha over a minor tactical training problem and the latter had mentioned it in his confidential report.

11 September. Another evening with the Mithas. Stimulating talk about ideas and a life of leisure; how he would love to visit England and would welcome me to Pakistan again. More on his experiences in Burma where he was critical of Wingate's (second?) expedition because it was poorly planned. He had met and admired the soldier-author John Masters, noted for his memoir *The Road Past Mandalay*.

14 September. A ghastly day that will always haunt my memory. Already feeling sick and very ill when I left Kakul with Akram at 6.45. Had to stop en route to be sick and go to the lavatory. A long wait in the C-in-C's office where I could not get a cold drink. At last in a half hour conversation with General Yahya and Mitha we discussed military history at the P.MA, Liddell Hart, and the Institute for Strategic Studies in London. Yahya could see that I was ill and called in the chief medical officer (another general). The latter diagnosed acute appendicitis and ordered Akram to take me to the military hospital at once for an operation. Whatever my ailment I knew it was not appendicitis: an operation would surely kill me.

I somehow managed to begin an interview with the Chief of Staff but was too ill even to stand and had to cut the meeting short. Akram faced an awful choice between his loyalty to me and his direct order from a very senior officer. I persuaded him to take me to the British Council offices where I could hope to rest. If I was no better in twenty-four hours then he could take me to hospital. It was not until about 11.0pm that I got to bed – in William Flemming's flat, a generous gesture on this young British Council official's part which probably saved my life. At the worst I could not even keep a tablet down. I recall watching a gecko on the ceiling and wondered if I would ever see Medmenham, and my happy home, again. The next day I was able to take a sleeping tablet and was knocked-out for several hours. I noted at the time that this was probably the worst illness of my life, the extreme discomfort exacerbated by the belief that I had messed up what should have been the climax of my visit, and also by the intense heat – 99° in Rawalpindi. After another day's rest I was driven back to Kakul in the head of the British Council's Zephyr where he discussed the possibility of my coming out again in the following March.

16 September. Another friendly talk with Mitha when he told me he was determined to visit Britain, at his own expense if necessary: his eventual ambition was to gain a post at University. However, my talk on Clausewitz in the evening did not go well because Mitha kept interrupting and ended the meeting simply by walking out, only to continue a boring harangue in the ante-room. This was a less attractive side of Mitha which I was to witness again.

18 September. Another late night discussion with Mitha in which he claimed to be an existentialist, throwing names around with gay abandon. On this visit I was more impressed by Mrs Mitha than her husband. She is well-educated and has a good mind but probably is not interested in 'shop talk'. I noted that Mitha seemed almost as much impressed by me as I was by him. Despite his faults he is a charismatic leader and I now (2017) think I have since only met one more entrancing personality; namely Leonard Cheshire who came and lectured to my students.

19 September. At P.MA I gave an evening lecture on 'The Military Intellectual'. This should have been 'right up Mitha's street' but he was boorish in manner and terribly rude to the Director of Studies. He propped up the bar until very late in the evening when I managed to escape – a disappointing end to my stay in Kakul. The next day I was driven back to Rawalpindi with William Flemming in a High Commission car.

21 September. Gave an early morning lecture to the CGS and the top brass at GHQ where I think the topic was 'Limited War'. There were some questions, naturally from the Pakistani angle, but I recorded the CGS's comments as 'brilliant'. General Yaqub Kahn was indeed a brilliant man whom I was fortunate later to invite to my home and take to meet Liddell Hart, where we were photographed on the lawn. His post-Army career was indeed brilliant. He was Foreign Minister 1982–91 and 1996–7. He died in 2016 aged 95. I also

discussed my report with the Director-General of Military Training who was not a fan of Mitha and seemed lukewarm about my proposals for the P.M.A. Later that day I had a long interview with the CGS who elaborated on his ideas about 'operational strategy' a concept which he felt was neglected in Britain and the United States. He impressed me as on par with the best European and American strategic thinkers and I was flattered to be the recipient of such frank personal opinions.

22 September. I flew to Lahore where I was made welcome by Mr and Mrs SA Bukhari, who put me up in their 'castle like' home. They were very friendly and took me on an extensive tour, including the famous Shalimar Gardens where I noted critically that the water was stagnant and there were no flowers. Alas, I did not properly enjoy their well-meant excursions because it was 92° in my fan-cooled room and 103° outside. Even a solar eclipse did not impress me.

23 September. My big lecture at Government College was my only opportunity to show appreciation to the British Council for my travel grant, but it was a disaster. At the heart of my trouble was my choice of title: the history of the 'Just War Tradition' looked alright in London, but appeared quite different in Lahore where the term signified war against unbelievers, and hostility to India. The Principal, whom I disliked at once, gave me a mini lecture on what I should say ('a load of rubbish' I noted), and then kept me waiting at the lectern with a long-winded introduction. This was only the start of my troubles: in a vast auditorium there was no microphone, no water on the lectern, and such poor lighting that I could barely see my notes. As soon as the audience got the drift of my academic argument students began to file out. I found this distracting and called a halt: they should leave now or sit still. Many left. I did my best but, apart from all the practical problems, the audience was palpably hostile. The students' questions or statements were mostly anti-American and intended to make me denounce the Vietnam war, while the staff's attitude was even more critical. At the post-lecture meeting one of the professors openly insulted me while others were sullen. This atmosphere continued throughout the lunch. I was sorry about the embarrassment I had caused to members of the High Commission and the British Council, but believed that I had had no choice but to defend myself against what I regarded as unprovoked bad manners. I feared that I might have caused a diplomatic incident.

Proud Borlase boy and father, 1948.

Head Boy with prefects, Borlase School, 1953-4.

2nd Lt Bond with E Troop 12th LAA Rgt, Germany, 1956.

Madeleine, my future wife, in a field near Medmenham, 1960.

Basil and Kathleen Liddell Hart with my father on our wedding day, 1962.

Liddell Hart and his 'Rogues' Gallery'.

Sir Michael Howard, Regius Prof at Oxford, 1980 (From *Captain Professor*, courtesy of Sir Michael Howard)

Professor Peter Simkins, President of the Western Front Association, and a friend for more than 50 years. (Courtesy of Professor Peter Simkins)

With my mother, Olive Bond, in Trafalgar Square, 1959.

With Michael Howard at States House, c. 1974.

Brian with Madeleine and Sable at Olmeda.

Brian with Japanese friends Professor Yasuyuki Kawamura (page x) and Tomoyuki Ishizu (page xi).

Brian appointed a Fellow of King's College, London, 1996.

Brian and Madeleine at All Souls College, Oxford, 2000.

The Post Office at Medmenham, c. 1900.

The Dog and Badger Inn at Medmenham.

My father c. 1969, teatime at States House.

Basil and Kathleen Liddell Hart, Davis, California, 1965.

On the next day I had a leisurely journey (by coach I think) to Quetta via Lyallpur and Multan. No one met me at the terminus; the officer who eventually collected me was unfriendly saying the mix up was all PMA's doing; while the librarian with whom he left me spoke little English and had had no notice of my visit.

On 25 September I was given a long tour up the Khojak Pass to the Afghan border and taken briefly across it at Chaman. My escorting major was surly and there was little conversation during the whole exhausting journey.

On 26 September I gave a seminar to the senior officers' War Course on 'The Role of the Military Intellectual' which stimulated good questions and further discussions over tea. In the evening I lectured to a large audience on 'The Indecisiveness of Modern War', which I felt had gone over well though there were only a few questions. I had given a similar lecture at the Wright-Patterson Air Force Base at Dayton Ohio the year before in a vast auditorium.

On 27 September I flew to Karachi where I stayed overnight with a friend of David Chandler's, Bruce Powell and his wife, who took me to the coast where we watched a great shoal of fish being trapped in nets. Bruce saw me off at noon on 28th and after an 11 hour flight arrived home in the evening. My somewhat banal concluding thought was how rapidly impressions fade as one returns to one's daily way of life. An impression which did not fade, however, was the appalling treatment of ordinary women who were treated as second-class citizens if their existence was recognised at all.

The aftermath of this demanding trip was an anti-climax. I was not invited to Pakistan again and, in view of the somewhat severe bout of jaundice I suffered on my return I was not too upset. I continued a long correspondence with Mitha but never saw him again. He was promoted to Major-General and appointed Quartermaster General but my belief is that, as regards the transformation of the P.MA, his radical, Western-influenced reforms were blocked by conservative senior officers. He left the Army in 1971 to become a chicken farmer; an unglamorous denouement for such a dynamic leader. He died in 1999. My brief visit, however, was not entirely in vain. Major Akram successfully completed the King's MA course in War Studies in 1970 and paved the way for a long succession of able Pakistani officers, airmen as well as soldiers. They enlivened our courses and doubtless had a positive influence on their return.

2 – Canada, 1972–3

I spent an academic year 1972–3 on sabbatical at the University of Western Ontario (UWO) at a much more provincial London than I was used to. I was pleased with this appointment. My title was Visiting Professor of Strategy in the History Department; it was a welcome break from routine; with all the challenges of a country and university I had never visited before. In retrospect I have no regrets about my time in Canada and believe I made the best of my opportunities. If my stay was not as comfortable or enjoyable as it might have been that was due to three reasons.

First, I was by myself most of the time. Madeleine came out for a few weeks to get me settled in, and how glad I was of her help, but then had to return home to look after our beloved English setter, Sheba. Secondly I found lodgings on the ninth floor of an apartment block surrounded by other blocks with only a glimpse between them of distant fields. This was about two miles from the university so I bought a huge Pontiac to drive to the campus. Thirdly, I was there through the winter months when the weather was, I suppose, normal for Canada but depressing for me. There were a few bright, sunny days but the usual pattern was snow, rain, slush and more snow. At its iciest the wind was much sharper than anything I had known in southern England.

My loneliness was mitigated by several friendships, two in particular deserve special mention for their warm companionship and helpfulness. Dr Roger Emerson, a bachelor from Vermont, taught in the History Department where his special interest was the Scottish Enlightenment in the 18th century. I saw him almost every day and had a meal in his cosy flat about once a week. He helped me to acquire the car, collect my luggage from the airport and see me off when I left. My other close friends, from an adjacent block were a Scot, Sandy Craig, who taught at the university, and his wife, Joanne, who was a doctoral candidate in English Literature, specialising in Edmund Spenser's *The Faerie Queen*. I visited their apartment regularly to watch television, discuss politics (they were well to the left of my position), and listen endlessly to a record of the songs from 'Oh What a Lovely War!'. Quite apart from the wine we consumed, and our conversation, I always left in an upbeat mood from those poignant lyrics.

If I mention that next to these three fellow tower-block dwellers my other closest friends were the American professor of journalism, Bud Wild, and a

Frenchman, Jean-Claude Vilquin, then it may seem that I found the Canadians unwelcoming. That was certainly not the case, but I could understand at the time, and even more in retrospect, that the historians had their professional anxieties about tenure and promotions. I was not going to be around long enough to cultivate deeper relations than occasional meetings at the Club or a party.

My duties were quite demanding but manageable, especially as I had most evenings to myself without a television so with ample leisure for reading, preparing lectures and marking essays. The last-mentioned were numerous because my main lecture class numbered about 35, with two smaller seminar groups, one of them a graduate class. The general education level was good but lacking the international mix and stimulus that I was used to in the other London. I was intrigued by one very young student whom I asked how he had qualified to wear his Harvard T-shirt. The question astonished him: he just liked the colour and the emblem. Another asked me if he could transfer 'spare' marks from a course where he had done well to another where he was borderline in order to 'major' in the subject. It was not on.

The great advantage I enjoyed as a visiting professor was that I was free from committees and admin so that I could arrange short breaks for travel. In the autumn term I only had three such excursions. Early in the term I attended, with my wife, a high-powered military history conference at Colorado Springs which I remember for two reason (though I did hear some excellent lectures): my luggage was missing for most of the stay, and I got horribly drunk. I attribute this uncommon lapse to two causes; the venue was about 12,000 feet above sea level and the gin and tonics were exceptionally strong. The frosty air as we emerged at midnight dealt me a knock-out blow. My wife somehow got me through the night and, belatedly, to the conference by noon the next day.

After Madeleine's departure I visited York University in Toronto to give a lecture for Al Tucker, who was one of less than a handful of scholars interested in the Victorian Army when I began research in the 1960s. At the Royal Military College at Kingston my host was an Australian, Peter Dennis, who would succeed me at U.W.O.

In the Spring Term I travelled a great deal but in most cases I need only mention the venues: Ohio State University at Columbus, already a centre for military history; McGill University at Hamilton; and Brockport College near Rochester, New York State. At Winnipeg my host was Robert J Young, whom

I had known when he was a doctoral student at LSE. The posters advertising my lecture, on the 1930s, were all illustrated with German tanks and my British affiliation was given as Kong's College, London, which provided a neat zoological opener.

It was a rejuvenating experience to arrive in Vancouver Island with Spring already evident in early February. There I lectured at Royal Roads Military College where I had a good friend in Al Wallis, a King's MA in War Studies and companion on several visits to Twickenham. At Victoria University I lectured without notes on Liddell Hart and felt it had gone very well. My hosts, however, left me 'high and dry' at the 'very posh' Empress Hotel when I needed to converse and wind down. Whenever possible I have tried not to leave speakers 'cold' on such occasions. Back on the mainland I spoke at a very lively seminar at Simon Fraser University and stayed with Martin Kitchen and his family. Martin, a former research student at Oxford with A.J.P. Taylor, was already an authority on German militarism and, equally congenial for me, a lover of modern jazz. This was a halcyon brief holiday with walks along the shore and in the forest.

If British Columbia had been a tonic after the drab winter landscape around London, then my lecture tour to North Carolina and Rhode Island in late March was a revelation. I was familiar with beautiful college gardens at Oxford, but the campuses at Chapel Hill and Duke University were enchanting in a different way; great expanses of sweeping lawns, majestic trees and white colonnaded buildings. Here was a glimpse of the Southern Spring at its freshest before the onset of summer heat.

At Chapel Hill I was frankly out of my depth because the programme required me to lecture on 'Arms Control in the Third World' on which, to put it mildly, I was an amateur. I would have got by with undergraduates but these were experts, some even authorities on the topic. It was 'just one of those things' and I can only recall that they were very polite. Duke was a strong centre for military history, headed by Theordore Ropp whom I have mentioned earlier as plunging me without warning to speak to his senior graduate class. I see on checking my diary that this ordeal began at 8.0am! Anyway I was confident on 'Liddell Hart'. There was a good discussion and I was lavishly entertained. On a delightful tour I was shown the spot where General Joseph E. Johnston had surrendered the last Confederate Army in April 1865. To my great regret this is my only visit to a theatre of the Civil War.

On my way back I visited the US Naval War College in a wonderful setting at Newport, Rhode Island. My initial contact was with Lieutenant John Hattendorf, a submariner, due to go to Oxford in 1973 to study for a PhD. John became a close friend on my subsequent visits to Newport (when not in England) and in Oxford over the next thirty years. He is still at Newport, where I last saw him in 2006, and is one of America's foremost naval historians.

One of the great 'might have beens' of my career concerns the Naval War College. In 1972 the new President of the College, Admiral Stansfield Turner, later head of the CIA, was bent on revolutionising the main courses by bringing them more into line with what he had admired as an Oxford Rhodes scholar. In particular he wanted to broaden the syllabus and encourage open discussion in which there was no 'staff solution'. I suspect he had been given my name by Norman Gibbs because I was certainly not well-known in the United States, if anywhere. He rang me at home and urged me to come over for a year to help start the new course. I told him I had just committed myself to U.W.O. to which his response was 'whatever they are paying you, we'll double it'. Alas, I could not renegue on a signed contract, but he agreed that I could make annual visits for as long as I liked. I did indeed make further visits for three or four years (with other European scholars), before it was decided that these lectures could equally well be given by Americans.

I shall always think of Newport, the town and the College, with great affection. Visiting speakers were lodged in luxurious cabins on a splendid yacht moored on the quay within walking distance of the College. Excellent meals were served there and it was comforting to lie at ease listening to the roaring wind and the waves rocking the boat. Lectures and seminars to the best and brightest naval officers were a stimulating challenge with a first-rate academic staff who struck me as a true 'band of brothers'. I remember some of the other visitors, including Marten Blumenson and David Ralston, both distinguished historians, and permanent staff such as Ken MacDonald, Craig Symonds and David Hicks. One year I came over in early November when the New England fall was at its most brilliant and was privileged to be taken on a day tour to Concord to visit nearby Walden Pond where Henry David Thoreau had built and lived in his famous hut between 1845 and 1847.

Despite the drawbacks I mentioned earlier, especially loneliness at weekends, I had enjoyed teaching my classes, reading in the excellent library, meeting people in the Club at lunchtime and relaxing with my tower-block friends in the evenings. I liked what I saw of Canada and Canadians and only wish I could have seen more of this exhilarating country at its summer best. I did return twice to Kingston for conferences but never saw London, Ontario again. U.W.O. had been a brief but important episode in my career, and I remain grateful to all the individuals who went well beyond the bounds of normal sociability to ensure that I had a memorable time.

3 – Israel

I made two brief visits to Israel, in 1975 and 1982, the former alone to conduct interviews for my book on Liddell Hart, and the latter with a small group of academics interested in recent Israeli history and defence problems.

My first day in Israel, on 10 September 1975, could not have gone much worse. The security officials at Lod airport decided to give me a thorough going-over, scattering my luggage on the floor and insisting I tell them who I was going to meet. They would not accept 'some people' so I had to give them a list: the prime minister, foreign and defence ministers and other well-known public figures. 'So you call them some people' was the response.

My trouble was only just beginning. I expected to be met by my former MA student, Chaim Bar-on, but no one showed up. I was very worried because I had little money and did not even know which city to go to. I took a taxi to Jerusalem and found very cheap lodgings. I rang Bar-on at intervals through the night and at last made contact. He had been ordered on military duties at short notice and had asked a friend to meet me. He transferred me to an unfinished hotel in a barren area outside the city. Bar-on was busy and it was Yom Kippur so there was no food at the hotel and no public transport to get out. Here my luck changed in that I had been given the phone number of Ruth Connell, widow of the late John Connell – military biographer. She was the editor of a Jerusalem newspaper but was convalescing at home after an eye operation so was at leisure to put me up and give me meals. This was a cosy haven for the weekend after the turmoil of the previous days.

I returned to Tel Aviv where Bar-on, to his credit, had arranged the interviews I had asked for. These were made possible because he was a senior secretary in one of the ministries, the Foreign Office I think. I had already interviewed the brilliant strategist and archaeologist, Yigael Yadin in London and now, in their

Tel Aviv offices I met Yitzhak Rabin, currently prime minister, Yigal Allon, who had described Liddell Hart as 'The Captain who teaches Generals', and Haim Laskov, who had served in the British Army and was a keen reader of Liddell Hart's books. All were polite and as helpful as possible but my line of enquiry was a difficult one; what, if any, influence had Liddell Hart exerted on their military ideas, policies and actions? One person's 'influence' on another is very hard to assess and Basil was very keen to claim that he had been an important influence on successful strategists and commanders, particularly Germans and Israelis.

Liddell Hart's visit to Israel from 20 March to 5 April 1960 as a guest of the Government was something of a triumphal tour. He was hailed by the Press as 'the greatest military expert of our time', 'the Clausewitz of the 20th Century' and 'the Pope of theory', while he in return was quick to laud his hosts as his best disciples and the most brilliant soldiers in the world. He had interviews with all the 'top brass', including discussions over the map with Laskov and his Vice Chief, Rabin, and with the Prime Minister, Ben Gurion. He also gave five public lectures which some people found disappointing. Journalists were clearly puzzled by his appearance which in no way coincided with their image of the bluff, red faced, thickset British officer. One journalist delightfully characterised his somewhat incoherent manner of speaking:

> He is a very charming man. In spite of his 65 years, he still stands erect, showing his full height, and what a height – almost 2 metres… A gold watch chain decorates his waistcoat, a pipe never moves from his mouth and he speaks – but that's a story in itself – he swallows every word, skips half a sentence and finally – repeats himself. That is the famous Cambridge style of speaking, a vestige of a Golden Age of the British Empire.

One suspects on this brief but hectic tour that the Israelis gained less from Liddell Hart's public pronouncements than from his genius at stimulating individuals and provoking them to fresh thought. This was certainly the impression of one of his most brilliant disciples, Dr Israel Beer, a leading military historian and commentator who had chaired one of Liddell Hart's lectures, and wrote a few days after his departure:

> I think that visit and your lectures have done a lot of good to our officers and the results will be felt in our Army sooner or later. You have forced many people to use their brains again, people who have become lazy, too spoiled and arrogant by successes, whose real causes they do not completely understand. You have by your work during your whole lifetime tried to infuse 'old armies' with dynamism and a flexible way of thinking. Believe me, that a 'young army' like ours, does even need more what you have to give, such as sound reasoning, penetrating analysis and above all your moral stature.

In trying to answer the extremely difficult question of how much influence Liddell Hart had exerted on Israel's military theory and practice I indicated that while it would be foolish to take the simplistic claims of certain journalists literally, it would be even more unjust to dismiss the formidable evidence in his support. In short, Liddell Hart received as much credit and praise for Israeli military achievements in 1948–9, 1956 and 1967 as any theorist and particularly a foreigner has the right to expect during his own lifetime. Doubtless had he still been alive in 1973 further tributes would have been forthcoming and possibly another signed photograph or two to join those of Yadin, Allon and Sharon in his study. The main point seems to be that his influence was mostly implanted indirectly, that is by means of his books, and articles, and most officers would meet these in translation or at second hand from lectures. In the 1940s Yigael Yadin was the crucial medium who transmitted Liddell Hart's broad thinking about war to a small but highly significant group of officers, several of whom, such as Rabin, reached key positions. In the 1960s a later generation of officers had the importance of the strategy of indirect approach impressed on them in university courses, in particular those of a whole-hearted follower of Liddell Hart at Tel Aviv, Professor J.L. Wallach. As regards armoured warfare, Liddell Hart's ideas were expounded chiefly by General Haim Laskov in the mid-1950s and early 1960s.

I used these interviews with much additional material from Basil's voluminous correspondence files in the final chapter of my book *Liddell Hart: A Study of his Military Thought* (1977) so need not elaborate here. Now I can only remember that Rabin gave me half an hour of his busy schedule but was very reserved; 'with all the charm of a rusty razor' was my note at the time. Ariel Sharon gave me longer and fully lived up to his popular image as a driving, ruthless field commander in the Rommel mode. I drew a blank, however in trying to draw him out on his view of civil-military relations, particularly as they affected his own career. It was almost as though the very concept was alien to him: he would act promptly and worry, if at all, about the political consequences later.

This visit was clearly of some significance for me. I had gained vivid impressions of Jerusalem and Tel Aviv; met the important people I had hoped to see, and learnt a certain amount about the successful Israeli military system. I briefly entertained hopes of returning to conduct research on the latter topic, especially their ability to wage sudden mobile warfare with a largely conscript army, but the opportunity never arose.

Instead, as mentioned earlier, I returned for a week in March 1982 in a group of about a dozen academics sponsored by a conservative political group keen to foster good relations with British opinion-formers. This worked well up to a point. We were given extensive tours of the country with visits to the Holocaust Museum, the Golan Heights and the Lake of Galilee. The price we paid for this hospitality was, however, steep. Every evening we were treated to a propaganda barrage of films and lectures stressing Israel's right to occupy all its present territory and even more disputed land. We were so irritated by this incessant brow-beating that eventually one of us, Dr Trevor Smith I think, stood up and explained that while in principle we had all come out as sympathetic to Israel and its problems this over-kill was likely to produce the opposite effect to the one required. I believe this served to modify things a bit, but of course the programme had been pre-arranged.

I did not go on the group outing to Masada but instead had a memorable day there with Uri Bialer and Michael Howard, who was making a personal lecture visit. In Uri's car we travelled via Jericho and the Dead Sea to the mountain fortress of Masada where we joined the queue for the funicular railway. An angry middle-aged lady sharply accused us of queue-jumping, and when Michael politely replied that we were in our rightful position she scornfully remarked 'You should learn some history'. I told her that she was addressing the Regius Professor of Modern History at Oxford but that did not seem to impress her. Perhaps I should have added that Michael was Jewish on his mother's side and knew at least as much as she did about the sufferings of her race.

The view from the summit of Masada was magnificent. Close at hand were the water caverns and grain stores which supported the Jewish resistance. The huge ramp which the Romans built to storm the citadel was still prominent as were the stone circles below marking the besiegers' camp. This remains not only a wonder of the ancient world but also a continuing symbol of national heroism. This visit, in congenial company, remains among my happiest memories of Israel.

4 – Greece and Crete, May 1991

In May 1991 Mike Dockrill and I attended a long and lavish international conference to mark the fiftieth anniversary of the German conquest of mainland Greece and Crete. This at first seemed a curious anniversary to commemorate but a hidden agenda soon became clear.

Since one of us had to 'mind the shop' at King's Mike very generously agreed to attend the first phase of the conference at Thessaloniki (Salonika) while I came out (with Madeleine) for the second phase, mainly held on a small cruise ship. While Mike was still there the party was taken by coach to visit the Metaxas line on the frontier with Bulgaria. I remember the impressive mountain scenery but no lecture to explain how the Germans had quickly broken through. Perhaps this had been discussed before I arrived, but the alleged heroism and the duration of Greek resistance here and in the centre of the country would soon cause a furious controversy.

On 24 May there was an all-day conference at the Eloundas Palace Hotel. Some of the historians addressed other topics, such as the campaign in Norway in 1940, but I spoke on the conference theme about the Allied defeat in Crete in May 1941 and this seemed to go down well with the audience. But when I chaired a lecture by Dr Horst Boog, an air warfare authority from the German History Research Office at Freiburg, all hell broke loose. Boog described the German drive through Greece as rapid and overwhelming. I think he used the phrase 'like a knife through butter' or words to that effect. His argument seemed entirely convincing to me: the Greek forces had excelled against the Italians and had no reason to feel ashamed at their efforts to stop the German *blitzkrieg* which had also swept aside the Allied (mainly Australian and New Zealand) contingents.

This version of events, however, was anathema to the Greek majority of the audience, and especially the organisers, a retired Admiral and his brother, who had encouraged a strikingly different interpretation. In essence this was a belief that Greece had 'won the Second World War' because her forces' prolonged resistance had delayed the German invasion of the Soviet Union (Operation Barbarossa) until 22 June, thereby allowing the Russians to delay the enemy advance until the harsh winter conditions saved them and enabled them to concentrate such huge forces that they could hold out and eventually roll back the invaders.

I could see little merit in this counter-factual argument, indeed it seemed to me an unhistorical myth. The German offensive had begun on 6 April, Thessaloniki had fallen on the 9th and Athens was reached on 27th. The surviving British and Greek forces had all evacuated the mainland by the end of April. I understood, furthermore, that any delay in launching *Barbarossa* had been caused by extensive flooding across areas of the assault sectors. Finally, on a wider view of the German failure in Russia, other errors, in strategy, logistics and assessments of the enemy's powers of resistance, seemed more significant than any 'friction' resulting from the conquest of the Balkans.

Consequently, I was unable to accede to the organisers' demands that I criticise Boog's paper; on the contrary I stated that in essentials I was in agreement with him. This did not go down well. Even in the lunch queue Greeks came up and reproached me for, in effect, siding with the enemy.

Later the two main sponsors of the conferences called a special meeting with Boog and myself. They had to communicate with the Greek media that evening and needed a positive story to report. We could not agree on anything positive about the Greek role in April 1941 but I had a bright idea. Why not focus on the Greek resistance, throughout their country including Crete, which truly had been sustained and heroic. 'Oh, we can't do that,' replied the Admiral. 'The resistance was led by the Communists and they killed my uncle.' Boog and I could not help further and had to leave the brothers to concoct a positive story that could be used by the Greek media. If I heard the outcome I have forgotten it; bravely though the Greeks had fought they had not even indirectly won the war in 1941 let alone 1945.

It would be ungrateful of me not to stress that the time spent cruising on our boat *Neptune* was delightful. We saw Mount Athos with its precariously-sited monasteries close-up, visited Lemnos and Santorini with its bay consisting of a vast volcanic crater. Then we cruised slowly along the north coast of Crete.

However, for a group of military historians, I did feel that too much time was spent visiting ancient monuments, sometimes just a few blocks of stone in a barren hillside, and not enough on what happened in the coastal towns, such as Heraklion and Retimo in 1941.

The climax of my discontent was reached when it was realised that our coach did not plan to stop when passing near Maleme on the way to a ceremony at Suda Bay. I had mentioned Maleme in my lecture as, beyond doubt, the key to the outcome of the battle for Crete. In their opening attacks on 20 May the Germans had suffered horrendous casualties among their paratroopers, and most of their gliders had crashed or been shot down. Unless they could seize, control, and open up an airfield for their troop reinforcements and supplies the whole operation might well end in a catastrophic defeat. For three days battle raged around Maleme until the Germans at last gained control and were able to use the landing ground. Historical controversy has lingered over this small but decisive episode because, thanks to Ultra intelligence, the British commander, General Freyberg, had advanced, very detailed information about German plans. He had insufficient troops to cover all the possible landing places so had to make hard choices. Did he give a sufficiently high priority to Maleme and its airfield? I thought not and was not convinced that he had deliberately neglected the area so as not to betray his secret source of intelligence gained from Ultra. But whether my views were right or wrong, it was surely essential that the party be given ample time to visit this confined battle area. In the event the coach driver was told to stop for twenty minutes, allowing myself, an Australian and a couple of others just time to run and scramble over rocks, look at the airstrip and hurry back again. This provided a disappointing insight into the organisers' priorities: plenty of time for ancient sites, cemetery wreath-laying and parades but very little for critical scenes of fighting.

In reflecting on this enjoyable yet frustrating tour I could understand why so much emphasis had been placed on the attempt at myth-making. Every nation needs its myths, especially those who have suffered humiliating defeat followed by brutal occupation. Even Britain needed its Dunkirk myth to muffle the impact of what had been a shocking defeat. Nevertheless where there is a long democratic tradition in politics and in robust academic independence, such myths can be constantly examined and criticised. I do not know enough about recent Greek history to offer a confident judgement, but from my very limited experience, I conclude that historians and journalists there must tread warily in challenging received wisdom.

5 – Germany

My national service in Germany had greatly stimulated my interest in the country and its history. I had seen a good deal of the British occupation zone (BAOR) including a moving visit to the concentration camp at Bergen-Belsen. On my way to Italy I had stayed at Heidelberg and Innsbruck with a diversion to call on a German girl in Rastatt-Baden whom I had met in England. That affair ended abruptly with a note under my door saying her father had forbidden her to see me again. She obeyed him and later, I heard, married an American officer.

In the late 1960s I got to see more of Cologne and the Rhine Valley through friendship with a young German student, Klaus Gütig, who had come to Medmenham to work in Liddell Hart's archive in preparation of his thesis. Unfortunately he had chosen a topic on which Basil was very sensitive and defensive; namely his writings on mechanised warfare theory in the 1930s which, he claimed, had significantly influenced German military leaders, especially Guderian, in their victorious campaign in 1940. The link between Basil's ideas and the *Wehrmacht's* operations were not so clearly documented as Gütig assumed, and when he persistently asked Basil where he should look next for the vital document the latter became irritated. Not surprisingly Gütig was somewhat disillusioned and, as far as I know, did not complete his thesis. This setback, however, did not affect our friendship which continued for several years.

Another good German friend was Professor Klaus-Jürgen Müller, who taught in Hamburg. Staying with his family I became fascinated by that great city's commercial history over the centuries. I talked to Müller's classes at the university and also lectured to the northern branch of the Staff College where, I am pretty sure, I met Claus von Stauffenberg's younger brother. Our friendship survived an awkward episode when Müller was staying with us. He had a rather obsessive interest in British military historians and how they were rated; almost as if we were in a league table ranked by points and even goal-difference. How did I rate myself in comparison with, say, John Gooch, and where would I place Correlli Barnett or Paul Kennedy? I had no objection to discussing individual's qualities and limitations, but this approach was too personal, so I asked him to desist.

I visited the Military History Research Office in Freiburg on several occasions in the 1980s and 1990s, attending conferences on aspects of the Second

World War or simply presenting a paper. I have already mentioned the conference when I was required to chair a session entirely in German. Of the many friends and colleagues there I will only mention Wilhelm Deist, Jürgen Förster and Manfred Messerschmidt. All in turn stayed at my home and spoke to my classes at King's or at the IHR seminar.

The main task of the impressive team of scholars at Freiburg was to produce the official history of Germany in the Second World War. Several volumes have been published but they are very long and massively documented. Even in translation they have not made a big impact in Britain. Förster was a member of the team which showed conclusively that nearly all the German generals commanding on the Eastern Front, including von Manstein, had been complicit in Nazi atrocities. He also told me that some families of senior Nazis were still in receipt of state benefits or profiting in other ways from services to the Third Reich.

For several years Jürgen was especially close to us because he displayed an impish sense of humour. For example, on a visit to Claydon House, a National Trust property, he and Madeleine played a loud duet on African drums which were strictly off-limits to visitors. I feared we should be reprimanded and thrown-out. We lost touch for a time when he married and, in error, gave me the wrong address of his new home in Berlin.

Wilhelm Deist was not only a fine historian but also a deeply religious man determined to play his part in demonstrating his abomination of the Nazi regime under which his father had served as a doctor. It was a great tragedy that he died comparatively young of cancer.

Manfred Messerschmidt was an eminent historian who had been just old enough to be conscripted into the anti-aircraft defences near the end of the war. Much later he was the senior historian on the German panel of experts who examined possible war crimes charges against Kurt Waldheim, Secretary General of the United Nations (1972–81) for his conduct in the Balkans in the Second World War. In 1994 the American Justice Department concluded that he had been involved in atrocities against Jews and allied soldiers, but by then he had retired.

Perhaps due to his war service or to his special interest in international law, Messerschmidt was obsessive about the criminality of the Allied bombing of Germany. I think at our first meeting at a conference in Sweden he had sidled up to me at the coffee break and remarked 'Y'know, Brian, Churchill and Harris were war criminals'. I made my disagreement very clear and that should have ended the matter. However when we were staying with him some years later, and he had taken us on a wonderful outing to Lake Constance and the Swedish enclave on the far side, he began the topic all over again with the same opening phrase. Madeleine and I argued with him for some time to no avail and I regret to say I lost my temper and used words which would not have been permitted in the House of Commons. Quite apart from all the practical and moral issues of the strategic bombing offensive, I contended that Britain could not then have been prosecuted for war crimes because she was on the winning side. A trifle cynical perhaps but brutally realistic. I cannot believe that Messerschmidt would have wanted Nazi Germany to win and so be able to implement its version of international law.

In 1992 and 2006 I also attended two international conferences at Potsdam, reading papers on Britain's experience with national service after 1945, and the way in which differing national interests fatally undermined the Allied (France, Britain and Belgium) resistance to the German offensive in 1940. On both occasions we visited Frederick the Great's palace of Sans Souci whose atmosphere struck me as melancholic and decadent, though I was pleased that the memorials to his beloved dogs were still prominent in the forecourt. By contrast the Cecilienhof Palace, where the Allies met in the summer of 1945, to sign the Potsdam agreement, still seemed right up to date (as though the delegates had only just left), and tourist-friendly.

I will end this section on a happier note with memories of my German MA student, Herbert Singer, who worked for a television company in Munich. He would cause amusement in my special subject class by always making the point whenever there were generalisations about 'Germany' that Bavaria was a proud and largely independent state. This made sense for the pre-unification of Empire in 1871 and even, to some extent, for the First World War when the armies of the great German states enjoyed some measure of autonomy. But it was hardly an identity to boast about in the Nazi era when the party's original centre of power resided in Munich.

Herbert's other memorable contribution to the seminar occurred when I remarked that someone we were discussing (Harold MacMillan perhaps) had 'had a good war'. 'Vat is dat' said Herbert in astonishment, 'How can you have a good Vor'. It suddenly struck me that he had made a profound point: it would have been very hard to have 'a good war' in Germany between 1939 and 1945 without being a Nazi or at least a conformist to the regime. After 1945 it would have been an advantage to have been an anti-Nazi and even better to claim resistance credentials. In view of Britain's great good fortune to have been on the winning side in 1945 I think there has been little reflection on the long-term repercussions of being defeated and occupied, particularly in Germany and Japan, where such a catastrophe had been unthinkable. I might add that very few people in Britain in 1940 believed that defeat was possible, but we know now that it could have happened.

Herbert struggled to pass the MA exam, but did so at the second attempt and, in gratitude to me for helping with his extended essay, invited Madeleine and myself to spend a few days at his home near Munich. The highlight of this visit, on 29 June 1999, was a trip to the home of Ernst Jünger, who had died only in the previous year aged 102. For the journey to the village of Wilflingen in Swabia, some two hundred miles west of Munich, Herbert borrowed his father's Mercedes. Jünger's house was not open to visitors but Herbert convinced the curator, not entirely falsely, that I was a British authority on this remarkable man. His very long career as warrior, author of a huge variety of books, and mystical philosopher had brought him international fame, attested to by the fact that both Helmut Kohl and François Mitterand had visited his modest home while in office.

At the time of my visit I was unaware that he had died only the year before, but I should have known because we visited his grave in the local churchyard. The inside of the house had been deliberately left unaltered, probably, because it would need re-organising before being officially opened to the public. The contents were spartan and rather like an ascetic's cell. I particularly remember the simple iron bedstead; his First World War helmet with the gaping hole where a shell fragment had nearly killed him; and the immaculate drawers full of butterflies which was another of his special interests.

Although I do not share Jünger's mystic exaltation of violence in combat or his fervent nationalism, I do admire his honesty and literary skill in depicting his own experience in the First World War, particularly in his most famous book *The Storm of Steel*, which deserves to be much more widely read in British university courses. I shall always remain grateful to Herbert for making possible what amounted to a military historian's pilgrimage.

6 – Japan

First impressions: Travellers familiar with the Far East may wonder why any introductory remarks are necessary, but Japan really is a foreign country where some things are done very differently. A summary of first impressions will serve to set the scene for more specific experiences during our five visits between 1999 and 2009.

The journey from Heathrow to Narita takes eleven or twelve hours; quite comfortable in business or first class but no fun at all in economy. The ministry of defence does not provide staff cars at the airport, or at any rate not for me, and friends are not allowed to use their own cars for insurance reasons. Two hours or more in a frequently stopping bus can make you very tired before your hotel is reached.

There is no need to stress that Tokyo is a vast sprawling metropolis that is at first daunting to newcomers used to quiet, open country. Japanese friends who have been given mini tours of the Chiltern hills where I live have expressed astonishment at the open fields and woodland. Where are the houses and the people? How can this landscape exist within forty miles of London they wonder.

Yet, as all visitors notice, the huge numbers of people who throng the streets are remarkably well-behaved, somehow contriving to allow individuals their personal space. Politeness and deference to customers is even more impressive in public places such as shops and lifts. Courtesy in wrapping and presenting even simple purchases almost constitutes an art form.

Punctuality in Japan is so much emphasised that it can strike Westerners as obsessive and disturbing. Quite recently a train driver killed several people in a crash because he was driving recklessly to make up for lost time, and that time was at most only a minute or two. Japanese, in our brief experience, excel at what the British Army terms 'rush to wait'; that is get to the rendezvous well before time, and then hang about. I have always prided myself in being punctual, but being rushed when there is plenty of time is irritating.

We knew in advance that one is expected to give presents to dignitaries such as directors and heads of department, taking great care to grade each gift in accordance with the rank or prestige of the recipient. Madeleine went to a lot of trouble to select a dozen or so presents for each visit and even then we had to improvise once or twice, for example by signing of copy of one my books which I had brought for reference.

Lest any of these remarks may sound critical I must stress that we were treated very generously in financial terms, partly perhaps because visiting academics were placed on the same remuneration scale as senior business men. As a corollary of the generous pay scale the visitor was in principle on duty throughout a customary twelve day tour. This could mean in practice that some short leisure breaks had to be given a professional 'fig leaf'. Inspection of some military installations provided a cover for our visit to Kyushu; while I was required to deliver a lecture at Sapporo before we could take a short break in Hokkaido. We were also generously entertained for most of the time when at leisure.

I quickly learnt that lectures in English would not so much be 'lost in translation' as made to sound incredibly prolix. A simple statement such as 'the king is dead' would seem to require a translation which went 'all round the houses'. Consequently a normal lecture to a British audience of, say, 20–22 typed pages would need to be cut to about 12, thus sparing not only the audience but also the speaker, who would otherwise be looking ahead and wondering how he could omit phrases without confusing the translator – something I have done more than once.

Causing embarrassment or loss of face is a perpetual risk in Japan. Just once or twice we witnessed Japanese officers treat subordinates in a humiliating way, and when asked why 'X' had been berated the reply might be 'he very bad man'. We were unwittingly the cause of a Japanese academic losing face when we offered him a meal which he did not wish to accept, fearing I believe that he would have to treat us in return. He fled from the dining room feigning illness but was then seen eating complimentary snacks at a reception. He knew that we knew he had deceived us.

Another disturbing practice I noticed was that conference organisers vetted questions presented in advance from the audience and selected a few which they decided would be acceptable to the panel of speakers and to themselves. I expressed concern about this method on the grounds that difficult or embarrassing questions might sometimes be necessary to promote a lively rather than a bland discussion.

I have to admit that I did not fully come to terms with Japanese customs on what constitutes good food and comfortable living. We were once taken to a noted restaurant at Arita on the island of Kyushu specialising entirely in tofu dishes which was a treat wasted on me. I also avoided raw fish whenever possible, but there was a real danger of causing offence.

As regards basic comfort, our host Tom Ishizu did his best to find Western-style hotels or ryukan with soft bedding, pillows and chairs but this was not always possible. At the National Defense Academy where I was the guest of honour at lunch we were supposed to eat sitting on the floor, but I managed to obtain low stools for us. I do not wish these remarks to be read as whinging. A large part of Japan's appeal to foreign visitors lies precisely in its unique culture. My concern was mainly professional: if I had continual indigestion and backache, and could not sleep in inflexible beds then I should not feel at ease on the platform.

I conclude this brief introduction by contrasting my wife's attitude to Japan with my own. Madeleine, who has had a lifelong feeling of affinity with the country, as though she may have lived there before, found Japan tremendously exciting whereas my reactions were more mixed and ambivalent for reasons which the following pages should exemplify. I shall always be grateful for the opportunities I had to visit this remarkable country and only regret that they did not occur earlier in my career when I would have been more energetic and resilient.

We owed our first invitation in October 1999 to the good offices of my former MA student Tomoyuki (Tom) Ishizu, then a researcher in the history section of the National Institute for Defense Studies (N.I.D.S.) and now a senior professor there.

The subject of the international conference was 'War and Peace in the 21st Century', but viewed from the perspective of war in the 20th century. I spoke on 'The Approach to Total War, 1890–1918'. Other speakers included Edward Luttwak and Robert O'Neill, but the one who remains memorable, for the wrong reasons, was Georgy Arbatov, a former KGB officer and more recently director of a research institute in Canada. He arrived on the platform a few minutes late, delivered a rambling lecture and remained clearly 'the worse for wear' throughout the day. He made a nuisance of himself to all the females he encountered, including my wife. Furthermore he ruined what should have been a delightful dinner with Tom and a colleague on the 53rd floor of the New Opera House. I have not heard a word about Dr Arbatov since: the Japanese do not take kindly to visitors who behave badly.

After the conference Tom took us to Nara and on to the largely unspoilt city of Kyoto where we visited the Golden Temple and several others which were still impressive despite the huge crowds thronging them. After an enjoyable but tiring day a visit to a Geisha theatre was too much for me; the display was beautiful but trying to eat with chopsticks while lying on one's side was very uncomfortable.

At the conference we had met another academic, Professor Yasuyuki Kawamura, who was to be a host and friend on future tours and a visitor to Medmenham. We felt privileged to be taken to his home for dinner, the only time this ever happened to us in Japan, but it turned out to be a rather tense evening because his wife seemed embarrassed, taking ages to unwrap the small gift we brought her, and looking very unwell.

On this first visit we had a completely unexpected experience which is still almost hard to believe. The celebrated Yasukuni Shrine, revered by nationalists, was within walking distance of our hotel in Ichigaya and Tom invited us to see its museum and art gallery. On arrival we were taken – without footwear of course – to the most secret shrine for a ceremony with the Shinto high priest. We stood respectfully while prayers were said for the spirits of dead soldiers (Japanese we presumed) and were then given sake and small presents. Tom had arranged this privilege for us through a friend but I wish I had been told in advance of this honour because I was very casually dressed.

That same afternoon I was taken to lecture (on Liddell Hart) at the headquarters of N.I.D.S. at Meguro-ku. This was like a little oasis in grim surroundings with its trees, birds and carp pool. Like London Tokyo has numerous 'villages' amid the urban sprawl. I made several visits to this venue and always enjoyed them, not only for the tranquil setting, but also for the courteous, though probing, atmosphere of the discussions.

This day ended perfectly with a dinner hosted by Tom at a French restaurant high in a tower block providing marvellous views over the city at night. The greatest pleasure however was to talk to six of Tom's bright, respectful young colleagues whose promising careers were about to start as mine was drawing to a close.

Our second visit, in September 2000, was not quite so enjoyable for one particular reason. I had agreed to give a series of six lectures to Kawamura's officer cadets at the National Defense Academy, which has an attractive setting on Tokyo Bay. The lectures were to be based on my book *The Pursuit of Victory* which Kawamura had translated into Japanese. So far so good, but the drawback was that he had booked us into an absent colleague's flat in a huge, soulless marina at Zushi where there was nothing to see or do.

Consequently we spent about a week there, reading and dozing until late afternoon when we were collected and driven to the Academy. I remember only one incident from the lectures which, I suspect, were over the heads of the cadets because they assumed a good knowledge of European history. In dealing with the tricky topic of victory and defeat in the Second World War I rather riskily suggested that Japan's defeat had turned out to be a sort of blessing in disguise because a militarist regime had been overthrown and a brief, benevolent American occupation had paved the way for a prosperous, liberal democracy. This jeu d'esprit was met with a stony silence until a last a senior officer stood up at the back and said that he completely disagreed with me. All Japan's problems, past and present, were entirely due to the United States. I restated my case and told him bluntly that he was wrong. The course ended with the customary dinner with generous praise from the President, so I hope no lasting offence was taken.

In retrospect the dreary days at Zushi dominate my memory but our hosts did make great efforts to entertain us on our free days. Professor Yoshinaga (Yoshi) Hayashi, Director of the Military History Department at N.I.D.S., and a former air force general, took us to dinner with his wife at a club. He and Raiko, both devout Roman Catholics, became good friends, visiting our home and even attending my farewell lecture at King's in 2001. We visited the famous temples at Kamakura and stayed briefly at a wonderful hotel called Kannonzaki on Tokyo Bay. Not only was there an impressive array of varied shipping endlessly in motion, but there were also colourful gardens and walks along the shore. However, the aspect of this very comfortable and expensive hotel that I treasure most was that in the lounge and dining room classical music was played. They only had a few records, Tchaikovsky, Brahms and perhaps Schubert, but this was still an unusual, civilised phenomenon.

The non-academic highlight of this visit should have been a weekend drive with Kawamura to the mountains at Hakkone with a chance of seeing Mount Fuji close-up. Unfortunately it was a public holiday so the roads were jammed and the journey tedious. Then we experienced heavy rain over the whole weekend. Kawamura did his best, taking us across a lake on a mock 18th century galleon, and to an art gallery, but Fuji remained mist-shrouded and unattainable. Back in Tokyo I gave other lectures that seemed to be well-received, but it is the lonely days at Zushi which remain uppermost in my memory.

Our third visit took place in January 2002 when the weather was surprisingly mild. We returned to Grand Hill Hotel, which I found comfortable and soothing, for a two day international conference which seems to have left little impression, though I noted good papers from Williamson Murray and Martin Van Creveld. On the third day Kawamura drove us down Tokyo Bay to Yokosuka and the Defense Academy where I lectured to a large audience. We rested and dined again at Kannonzaki but did not stay there, too costly I suspect for our hosts to afford.

On 19 January we flew to the island of Kyushu with Tom where we were met by a Colonel and staff car and driven to Ureshimo. Tom had found the most Westernised room for us at the ryukan in which, we were told, Emperor Hirohito had once spent the night. This reminded me of a visit to Zopot in Poland where we dined in the hotel used by Hitler in 1939, but in this case we were not even allowed to see his room. Back in Kyushu we spent a day at the fascinating pottery works and shops at Arita, but this is where I had the frightful lunch whose menu might have read 'anything you like so long as it's tofu'.

Back in Tokyo another good friend, Professor Imamura, whose curious special interest was mid 18th century European military thought, took us to the National Museum in a splendid park, and on to the Asakusa temple where I was touched emotionally by the large numbers of stray cats and a few dogs which were well fed by local people and tourists. A memorable day was completed by an excellent French meal with Kawamura and Imamura in the famous Ginza district.

There was a definite schedule behind our fourth visit in September 2002 where we again stayed at Grand Hill Hotel. On a day cruise to the Åland Islands during a conference at Stockholm I had a long talk with 'Yoshi' Hayashi about a future conference theme and suggested a comparison of British and Japanese combat performances in Malaya and Burma for which each of us would provide a small team. This idea impressed him and he obtained funding, but with the important proviso that the conference proceedings must result in a book published in English.

My team consisted of Mike and Saki Dockrill, Graham Dunlop, an ex-Colonel Royal Marines, who was writing his PhD at Edinburgh University on logistics in the Burma campaign, and Carl Bridge, head of the Menzies Centre for Australian Studies at King's College, London.

The two day conference went quite well on 18 and 19 September except for a mild spat with Saki. I had advised her that her paper was far too long for the tight conference time-table and needed to be cut a bit, but she insisted on reading every word. Whether this was the sole cause of her later animosity I do not know but on our return she refused point blank to give me any help with checking the Japanese papers before publication. The other aspect I noticed was the reluctance of Japanese speakers to be sharply critical of their military leaders even when, as in Burma, it was clear that calamitous mistakes had been made. This suggested very different approaches to the scope allowed to academics in exposing the failings of their leaders and institutions. I am glad to report that the book did get published with the title *British and Japanese Military Leadership* (Frank Cass, 2004).

As a sort of reward for my efforts in bringing this conference about I was able to pay a three day visit to Hokkaido, the northern island with its unique climate and terrain, which I was very keen to see. The only condition was that I lecture to a large military audience in Sapporo. This went off alright and we sat down to dinner with Kawamura and three generals at 5.30. Perhaps due to the language barriers it was a dull occasion which Madeleine tried to enliven by a slightly risky question which, alas, neither of us can remember. Perhaps she asked them what they would get for dinner since they would be home by 7.0pm. At about that time Kawamura went off to visit a friend so we were left alone, not for the only time, in a strange hotel. Here was a difference in Japanese social etiquette which we just had to accept.

Another social difference, which I have touched on earlier, occurred when we arrived back at Grand Hill Hotel after an exhausting journey. A librarian and his wife had invited us to dinner and a time had been agreed. We reached the hotel with half an hour to spare to wash and change, but there they were in the foyer looking as though they had been waiting for some time. Madeleine was furious with me but I 'pulled rank' and insisted we eat elsewhere since the hotel menu was unappealing.

This visit ended on a good note when Tom took us on another two-day trip to Kyoto. My main memory of this outing is not of the splendid temples, gardens and shops, but of a two hour headlong dash by canoe down rock-strewn rapids from a mountain top. The crews had done this many times but their dexterity was still remarkable. This was a brilliant improvisation on Tom's part and for once the weather was benevolent.

There was a long gap between this and our last visit in February 2009. Tom had secured funding at the last minute and sufficient for a week only. I had to bear all Madeleine's expenses which was fair enough. The hope and expectation was that if I made a good impression Tom would be able to invite us out again in the autumn with me as the keynote speaker at an international conference. We even planned with Tom the holiday we would take together afterwards. For financial reasons, perhaps complicated by changes of personnel at N.I.D.S. the conference did not take place, and we have not been invited since. Tom escorted us on a fascinating coach tour of the city, of which I remember a tea ceremony, a distant view of Mt Fuji from a high tower and lunch in gardens near the Imperial Palace. I then lectured, successfully I think, on Clausewitz at N.I.D.S.

On 19 February there was a strange incident that sheds light on the Japanese obsession with punctuality mentioned earlier. General Hayashi was giving us a wonderful lunch on the 25th floor of a grand hotel, but he was intentionally slow in ordering, knowing a staff car would be collecting me to give a lecture at N.I.D.S. The explanation behind this go-slow was that Hayashi was at odds with his successor at N.I.D.S. and meant to cause mischief by making us late. We had to abandon the meal mid way and dash for the lift. As we emerged Tom met us and raged at me for being *one minute late*! He was clearly afraid of a reprimand if we were indeed late at N.I.D.S. but there was plenty of time. That evening a small group of Japanese senior officers invited us to a very expensive meal which they had chosen without consulting me, the honoured guest, about the menu. I 'passed' on course after course of this meal and can only remember eating bread rolls and tempura. Did I lose face by this behaviour or was I 'more sinned against than sinning'?

The next day there was a similar incident over timing. Tom had taken us to an expensive shopping area near to the Meiji Shrine where Madeleine naturally took her time. Tom clearly got a call on his mobile, and told use abruptly that we had *seven minutes* for lunch. We grabbed something in a self-service bar and dashed to the staff car. We then waited for 40 minutes in the anteroom at N.I.D.S. with only a coffee to pass the time before my lecture. At least this received a standing ovation so that was a cheering end to what proved my last performance at N.I.D.S.

In addition to being much shorter than our previous visits this one was disappointing in another way. The financial support was less generous than before and we were placed in a very expensive hotel, the Shibuya Excel, where the cost of meals was prohibitive. For breakfast we went out to get a coffee and rolls in a café near the station, and made do with cheap, simple meals in the evening. Apart from the disastrous dinner mentioned above we were left by ourselves, Tom and Hayashi both having prior engagements.

On balance I would say that this final visit was a disappointment, bearing in mind that we were on the brink of being flooded when we left home and worried about the care of our cat. All was well in both respects. We had made the effort in good faith in the expectation that it would lead to an exciting follow-up in the autumn, so we must just be content that our four earlier trips had been very enjoyable and rewarding. If invited again after 2009 we would have been very pleased to accept, but now this Far Eastern adventure has surely come to an end.

12

Books do Furnish a Room

They also burnish a *curriculum vitae.* I have published a dozen books and edited as many more. This is not a bad output considering I have earned my living as a university teacher with responsibilities to undergraduates, graduates and doctoral candidates. I wrote most of my books to enhance my academic reputation rather than to try to reach a popular readership. To have survived on income from publications I should have had to change my style of life completely, and I am not sure that I could have done it. Quite apart from the time and physical effort required, I would also have been inhibited by the belief, perhaps mistaken, that I should only take on subjects which had been neglected, or where I thought I could make an original contribution to scholarship.

Inevitably there have been disappointments with some books I have published and with subjects that did not come my way, such as a full-scale biography. I was invited to write the biography of Field Marshal Sir John French but turned it down, partly because I did not admire him, partly because I thought there would be difficulties with his family. Richard Holmes overcame the latter problem and produced an excellent study – *The Little Field Marshal.*

In the 1960s I published a large number of articles, but was rather slow in tackling a book due to problems outlined in the earlier chapters. In 1967 I edited and contributed to *Victorian Military Campaigns*, discovering in the process that organising authors was as difficult as herding cats. I had to edit heavily and virtually rewrite some of the chapters and in retrospect wished I had written the whole book myself. I was conscious of the drawback that I had not visited any of the battle theatres discussed and that the approach was narrowly British. Nevertheless the book got some favourable notices, one reviewer calling it 'a gem', and I believe it helped to draw attention to an exciting and neglected subject, particularly the logistical problems of operating far from one's base, and of fighting in forbidding conditions against a succession of very different opponents.

My first proper book should have been a comprehensive study of the later Victorian Army on which I had concentrated for several years, but instead I contented myself with a narrower subject, *The Victorian Army and the Staff College, 1854–1914* (1972). I attempted to make this much more than an institutional history by treating the development of the Staff College as a touchstone for the radical changes in the whole military system in the period leading up to the First World War. In retrospect I regret that I did not tackle the much larger subject, but I never did any teaching on the Army in this era so there was no stimulus from students. More importantly, my interests were becoming more focused on the 20th century.

My experience with the diaries of Lt Gen Sir Henry Pownall (*Chief of Staff* 2 volumes 1972–3) was truly a lack of foresight saga. I was shown the twelve volumes of longhand diaries by a friend of the family while still at Liverpool University and asked if they were worth publishing. I had no doubt that they were and agreed to edit them. This intermediary then told me that I would be responsible for having the diaries typed and all twelve would be published by a well-known American firm with an office in London. I must have been very naïve indeed to accept this arrangement on trust. I am sure I never saw a contract or received any advance on royalties. I managed to get all the diaries typed inexpensively mostly by ex-secretaries of Liddell Hart, and carried out some basic editing. Alas, when I took them to the publishers they were completely dismissive, describing this huge typescript as 'garbage'.

In desperation I tried *Pen and Sword*, already an established publisher of military history, and there met my 'saviour' in the jovial form of Leo Cooper. Leo was a warm, unstuffy personality, a rugby fan and, above all, a genuine enthusiast for military history. Anything but a ruthless business man, he would take on books that he considered interesting, knowing that many would not cover their printing costs. This generosity more than once caused him financial difficulties but he was bailed out by his wife, the prolific and popular novelist, Jilly, who is happily still with us.

Leo agreed to publish the Pownall diaries in two volumes with the break after 1940 and before Henry became Chief of Staff to Mountbatten in South-East Asia. This faced me with very difficult decisions in reducing twelve volumes to only two, but I think it worked well. Any doubter or critic can check the originals in the Liddell Hart Centre for Military Archives at King's College, London to see what was omitted.

Pownall was a senior Army representative on the staff of the Committee of Imperial Defence between 1933 and 1938 when he became Director of Military Operations and Intelligence at the War Office. In 1939–40 he was Chief of Staff to Lord Gort, Commander of the Field Force in France, hence my title.

Henry Pownall used these diaries to 'let off steam' and so wrote extremely frankly about the defence problems and personalities in this critical period. Even when every allowance is made for impromptu comments and bias the diaries provide an invaluable source for these years. If possible he is even more acerbic about leading figures in 1939–40, especially French and Belgian generals, but these personal comments are offset by unique insights into the intense friction in the Allied command structure which contributed to the disastrous defeat.

I do not believe Leo Cooper profited from this publication, and I certainly did not, but it has brought satisfaction enough to see the diaries frequently cited by scholars of the period. One personal recollection may be permissible relating to Pownall's candid assessment of Lord Mountbatten in the second volume. While generally an admirer of his publicity-seeking chief, Pownall was aware of his shortcomings, including an alleged affair with a named woman serving at the command headquarters. I interviewed Lord Mountbatten in the hope that he might write a foreword to the second volume but his opening words were blunt and off-putting: 'I trust you do not intend to publish those remarks about me and Mrs X. They are untrue!' This section had been so heavily inked out that it was very hard to decipher, but clearly Mountbatten knew that the passage existed, although the diaries were in private hands. Needless to say, though courteous, he did not write a foreword.

Editing these diaries considerably deepened my understanding of the inner workings of Britain's defence institutions. Prior to this I had probably been too much influenced by Liddell Hart's standpoint as a critical outsider. The latter's detached standpoint had its advantages of course, permitting the journalist to speculate and advocate alternative policies while responsible only to his editor. Sir Maurice Hankey, Pownall and their colleagues were less gifted as original theorists than Liddell Hart, but they were privy to the latest intelligence and faced with day to day problems, involving political in-fighting and inter-Service rivalries which were not going to be resolved by an article in *The Times*. Even during his brief 'partnership' with the War Minister, Leslie Hore-Belisha in 1937–38, Liddell Hart could not be made privy to the innermost secrets of the defence decision-makers. Indeed this informal relationship infuriated some senior officers who understandably feared that a journalist was influencing important decisions.

My next book *France and Belgium, 1939–1940* (1975) was one in a series on British operations in the Second World War, but I had chosen the topic, which I was now teaching as a BA Special Subject. Editing the Pownall Diaries had given me a head start in understanding the personalities and issues involved, but I also read widely in British and French sources and also interviewed several survivors who had been involved in planning operations. The series editor stipulated that the book should be quite short and accessible to non-specialists, which suited me very well. I was able to concentrate on British and inter-Allied strategic planning and politics, intelligence about enemy intentions and, above all, the speedy unravelling of the Alliance under pressure of the German offensive in May 1940.

A seemingly humdrum but nevertheless important exercise was to establish precise details of when meetings took place and what had been decided. Diaries in particular had to be carefully checked because, under pressure of events, mistakes were often made. There were examples when Gort could not have been in two places on the same day, or Ironside (the C.I.G.S) could not have met French commanders as claimed. These were far from being trivial matters: such issues as when the Belgian Government (or King) sued for a ceasefire and when the Allies were notified; or when Gort decided to abandon the intended Allied counter-attack and make for the Channel ports, were of immense military and political significance. I had earlier, in a long correspondence, helped Guy Chapman whose study *Why France Collapsed* (1968) dealt with these matters, and the operations, in much greater detail than I was permitted. As for larger issues, I concluded that British participants (and especially Pownall) had been excessively critical of the Belgian role in the campaign; while the French had tried to 'pass the buck' to the British in attempting to mitigate their own major responsibility for the debacle. These bitter controversies continue to reverberate with each generation discovering them all over again.

When Basil Liddell Hart died suddenly from a stroke in January 1970 I was deeply shocked and saddened. As discussed earlier, he had been the key influence in shaping my early career and remained a father figure in all professional matters; indeed he once referred to me in company as 'more like a son than his own son'. This was a sad reflection on Adrian who remained a close friend. In practical matters Basil and I were contracted to produce a book together on the development of military thought from the 18th century, but I already had a feeling that he would not be able to fulfil his part, so in this respect his death was not a great disappointment.

For about four years I felt too emotionally involved with Basil to be able to write about him objectively, but then I thought of positive reasons why I ought to try. I knew him, his close family and many of his friends very well. I had read nearly all his books and was familiar with his career and its controversies. Indeed I was supervising an MA class on his strategic ideas on the day he died. Not least important, I lived within walking distance of his library and archives so could work there at leisure.

Lady Liddell Hart was most upset by my proposal. She wanted an important historian or public figure, such as David Dilkes who had impressed her by arriving at States House in a Bentley, and certainly not a little-known village boy whose father worked part-time in her garden. It was also pretty clear that she expected a hagiography which no self-respecting scholar would write. If I was *persona non grata* then an excellent alternative would have been my former PhD student, Dr (now Professor) Brian Holden Reid. Unfortunately Brian had given a lecture comparing Liddell Hart and 'Boney' Fuller stating, quite rightly, that one of them had been a fascist. Brian made it clear that it was Fuller and not Liddell Hart, but Kathleen convinced herself that Brian had implicated Basil and he too joined the outcasts. Eventually, many years later Michael Howard persuaded her that the right scholar to tackle the full biography was Dr Alex Danchev. He was another of my doctoral students: an extremely clever man with a florid style and remarkably wide interests in art, music and culture generally. He did not turn out to be the right choice though he produced a very favourable portrait pretentiously titled *Alchemist of War* (1998). He had never met Basil or other vital witnesses, was not at home with the historical context, and allowed his other interests to intrude in the text. The book also tailed off noticeably after 1945. Much later Michael Howard admitted to me that he had made a mistake.

In 1975, however, Michael had persuaded Kathleen that I should be allowed to write an interim study, leaving the field clear for a more distinguished biographer. There were three important conditions: the book must be published by Cassell where Basil's close associate, Kenneth Parker, could act as watchdog; it must be completed in one year; and it must be confined to Basil's books and ideas, leaving the rounded biography to another author.

These restrictions actually did me a favour, because Basil's private life was not all that interesting, while the evolution of his career and his thinking on war badly needed a concise analysis and critical commentary.

I delivered the typescript to Cassell precisely on time but then it lay on editors' desks for nearly a year. I asked my agent about the delay and he explained that the book could not go ahead without an American publisher. I pointed out that there was no mention of this in the contract and asked him whose side he was on. When he said that he was a sort of middleman between author and publisher I ended our relationship.

Liddell Hart: A Study of His Military Thought duly appeared in 1977, and with simultaneous publication by Rutgers U.P. in the United States. It was widely reviewed with all but two notices concluding that I had struck a fair balance between personal connections and objective analysis. This was more difficult to achieve than most of the readers could have known, but I was pleased that most of them did not think I had 'pulled my punches'.

The two exceptions noted above were John Terraine and the Marquess of Anglesey, who were not particularly hostile to me but rather used their reviews as a platform from which to attack Liddell Hart (see Appendix). These were the only two reviews Kathleen ever mentioned, as though I had deliberately set the stage for attacks on her husband. Although she remained friendly, even affectionate, in letters and conversations, she never really forgave me until, on her death bed at the age of 99 she more or less admitted that she had made a terrible mistake. Better late than never but she had rejected Bond and Holden Reid only to end up with Danchev. I hope that Brian Holden Reid will eventually produce a biography that will be as nearly definitive as can reasonably be hoped for.

British Military Policy Between the Two World Wars (1980) is the most thoroughly documented and scholarly study I have written. I was very fortunate to have as my editor at O.U.P. Dan Davin, a New Zealand officer wounded in the battle of Crete and author of *Crete* in the *Official History of New Zealand in the Second World War*. Dan was far too senior a delegate at the Press for this task but took it on because he had been a friend of Liddell Hart. Needless to say he did a thorough editing job but what I remember is his approbation of my critical comments on Neville Chamberlain and appeasement shown by emphatic remarks in the margins.

My broad aim in this volume was to demonstrate that the Army really was 'the Cinderella Service' between the two world wars. More specifically I tried to show that although the Army's military leaders were undistinguished they were not primarily to blame for their Service's unpreparedness at the outbreak of war and the debacles in May 1940 and later. From the time of Hitler's advent to power in 1933 the Committee of Imperial Defence and its sub committees had warned that Germany should be regarded as Britain's 'ultimate enemy' with the likelihood that an Expeditionary Force would have to be sent to Europe in support of allies. Few senior officers were keen on such a commitment and for ministers responsible for defence the prospect of another 'war in the trenches' was anathema. The Army could not be equipped and trained for Continental war without a clear political directive and this was not given until February 1939. Whether or not my book has altered historians' views on this controversy I do not know, but I have not seen my evidence and arguments seriously challenged.

In 1982 I was invited to edit the diaries of Walter Guinness, later first Lord Moyne who was assassinated in Egypt by the Stern Gang in 1944. There was no financial incentive but the diaries were worth publishing for the insights they offered on the career of a senior staff officer on the Western Front who was also an active Member of Parliament. The diaries were in a disorganised state, but the difficulties in editing them were more than offset by the opportunity to make several visits to Biddesden House in Wiltshire, the home of Bryan Guinness, second Lord Moyne. Biddesden had been built circa 1704 for one of Marlborough's generals, John Richard Webb and remains the most beautiful English mansion I have ever seen.

Lord Moyne was a welcoming host but had the disturbing habit of finding more pages of the diary when I thought what I had found was all that remained. Though happily re-married, I formed the impression that he had been permanently shaken by being deserted by his first wife, Diana Mitford, who had abandoned him for the dubious charms of Sir Oswald Mosley.

The interior of Biddesden House was as elegant as its enchanting Queen Anne exterior, but the Moynes' style of living was spartan. When my wife and I stayed there for a few days I shivered while the family seemed used to the cold. Our bedroom window could not be properly closed and our request for an electric fire was met with astonishment, though I believe an ancient model with one bar was eventually found. Also, despite the family's fortune in brewing Guinness, Lord Moyne had prohibited the consumption of alcohol in the house so meals were washed down with water or tomato juice. Nevertheless the aesthetic rewards were ample compensation for these minor discomforts: rooms filled with wonderful paintings and the magical view of the front of the house from the long entrance drive. The diaries were eventually published by Pen and Sword in 1987 under the title of *Staff Officer*. My then research student, Simon Robbins, was credited as co-editor for his work in compiling biographical notes on all the senior soldiers mentioned in the text.

My next book was the last in a series (to date anyway) on *War and Society in Europe* with my volume (1984) covering the century 1870–1970. I was very pleased to be invited to write a survey study aimed at a broad non-specialist readership. I felt comfortable with the 'warfare' aspect but unsure how to deal with 'society'. As a military historian I decided that war must take centre stage with its social dimensions in the supporting role. This differed sharply from the Open University's approach which focused more on social issues during and as a consequence of war.

I also had a problem with drawing conclusions which appeared true at the time of writing but might be rendered obsolete by global changes especially as regards nuclear weapons. The editor of the series, Professor Geoffrey Best, was unhappy with my final chapter and proposed drastic revision, but as our differences were mainly matters of opinion I insisted that my version should stand.

I was granted a sabbatical for the academic year 1992–3 and was elected a visiting fellow at Brasenose College, Oxford. I decided to complete a book exploring a large but neglected theme in military history. Inspired by the late Richard Holmes' work I chose *The Pursuit of Victory* as my topic, covering the period from the late 18th century to the present. On consulting the word 'victory' in numerous works of reference I found the accompanying qualification was nearly always negative such as 'futility of', 'pyrrhic', 'ephemeral' or 'deluded quest'. This dismissal truly represented liberal assumptions after the two world wars and the fear of nuclear annihilation, yet for the most of the period I covered achieving 'victory' was the unapologetic aim of belligerents. Of course as Robert Southey's famous poem 'After Blenheim' questioned, it was seldom easy to discover 'what good came of it at last', but I produced evidence to show that victory in battle had sometimes achieved lasting results. For example, Argentina has not as yet attempted to overthrow her failed invasion of the Falklands in 1982. A different but very important aspect of this question is that avoiding defeat, no matter how far falling short of war aims, is always preferable to losing.

My guiding star in this study was Carl von Clausewitz's great pioneering work *On War*, though I readily admit that some of his ideas and assumptions are no longer applicable. I mentioned earlier, in the section on Japan, that my book had been translated into Japanese and was apparently very popular there. I cannot understand why because I showed no sympathy whatever for that country's drive for victory in Asia between 1931 and 1945. Perhaps the translator added a gloss or interpretation which distorted my meaning. In any case I do not believe I have left any unexploded devices which could reignite the pursuit of victory as an openly declared national objective.

In the year 2000 I achieved two of my dearest ambitions: I was elected (albeit only briefly) a Visiting Fellow at All Souls College, Oxford, and delivered the Lees Knowles Lectures at Trinity College, Cambridge.

All Souls lived up to my high expectations in most respects. One disappointment however was the lack of academic events in my field in the evenings, so I decided not to take up the flat allocated to me in Iffley. Instead I would have dinner in College before taking port in the Common Room with its enchanting view, especially in winter, across the Hawksmoor quadrangle to the university church and the battlements of Brasenose. An even more magical experience, weather permitting, was to converse in the Fellows' Garden, about such profound matters as Inspector Morse's Oxford, until nearly midnight and then drive home at speed on deserted roads.

In these few months I prepared the four Lees Knowles Lectures. Sir Lees Knowles (1857–1928) was a barrister, Conservative MP and supporter of numerous worthy causes. He had a special interest in the Napoleonic era and became an authority on Napoleon's exile on St Helena. In 1912 he founded at Trinity College, Cambridge (his alma mater) a Lectureship in Military Science which continues to honour his memory. The lectures have been given annually, with a few gaps, by distinguished soldiers such as Field Marshals Wavell, Ironside and Slim; by scientists such as Sir Patrick Blackett and Sir Solly Zuckerman; and by historians such as Sir John Keegan, Sir Harry Hinsley and

Sir Michael Howard. I compiled a list of the lectures and their subjects for an appendix in my book.

Trinity College provided elegant lodgings for myself and Madeleine, and we arranged to stay there during the lectures: two in one mid-week and two the next. All went well for the first two lectures, but then the Thames rose rapidly and it looked certain we would be flooded. Consequently I had to dash off at about 7.0am and take a side lane across fields in order to get the car out. I left in such a hurry that I thought, wrongly, that I had forgotten my shoes and lecture notes. I rang my wife regularly through the day and night and was reassured that the water had not entered the house. On my return I could not get the car to the cottage, but the water level had dropped so we brought the furniture and carpets downstairs, only for it to rise again two weeks later and flood all the downstairs rooms. This rather dampened my memory of the lectures, but they stimulated lively discussions and were quite well attended. Some of my friends and former students, including John Lee, Peter Simkins, Gary Sheffield and Tony Hampshire, made a special effort to hear the lectures. Tony and I enjoyed a memorable after-dinner celebration in a private room with just two Trinity College dons, Denis Green and Robert Neild.

Cambridge University Press published my lectures as *The Unquiet Western Front* in 2002 and the paperback edition sold well. Even then success was rather clouded by misfortune. C.U.P. and Trinity College arranged a launch party to celebrate publication but I was in too much pain with kidney stones to attend. Fortunately there was a *deus ex machina* in the person of my old friend, Correlli ('Bill') Barnett, who had proposed me for the lectures and attended them all. Bill gallantly stepped in and, I feel sure, gave a more polished speech than I would have done.

Six years later, and now well into retirement, I published the book *Survivors of a Kind: Memoirs of the Western Front* which I most enjoyed writing. Many of the survivors featured, including Sassoon, Graves, Blunden, Manning, Chapman and Carrington, had been regularly discussed in my lively MA class so I was very familiar with their works. Who could write a dull book about such fascinating characters? Not me I hope. I also indirectly put a good deal of myself into these essays, for example, in mentioning places described in the memoirs and visited by me. A vivid example would be Edmund Blunden's melancholy reflections on revisiting Kemmel Hill overlooking the Ypres battle area and facing the grim truth that he could never throw off these ghastly memories.

I had received a modest advance on royalties, but low sales left me in considerable debt to the publisher. I had been persuaded to sign up for this firm, not at all noted for military history, because a young editor, who had been helpful to me at O.U.P., joined it with a mission to build up this speciality. Michael Howard also wrote for them with a similar experience to mine. My friendly editor left before my book was published and the effort to sell copies and get reviews lacked impetus. As well as hoping the book would sell well, I naively thought that it might generate interest in war memoirs as a comparatively neglected area of study, particularly if the scope was extended to cover famous non-British authors such as Barbusse, Jünger and Remarque. The book has been praised by authors and other publishers but that is all. I have now recovered the copyright.

In 2014 I published what was intended as a provocative study entitled *Britain's Two World Wars Against Germany* which would fit naturally into the public debates just opening up on the centenary of the war. I argued, not too polemically I hope, that in some respects, contrary to the general view, Britain had done more towards winning the war in 1918 than 1945. It seemed to me that although some historians had touched briefly on this comparison none had written even a short book on the subject. I regarded my effort, not as the equivalent of a doctoral thesis, but much more modestly as a pioneering exploratory essay which would surely provoke a heated debate. I expected some hostile reviews but was genuinely interested to see what line these would take.

The outcome has been a bitter disappointment which is still so painful that I am reluctant to open old wounds. I now believe that I chose the wrong publisher, given the combative approach noted above, and I certainly did not expect sub editors to require that virtually every statement should be footnoted. What complicated the checking process beyond belief was that our home was so badly flooded (the worst since 1947) that we could not live there between early February and late June 2014. Even when access became possible I could not physically get into my study to check references. As if all this was not bad enough, including a copy of the draft lost in the post, it looks as though few, if any review copies, were sent out. Consequently a book in which I had boldly gone out on a limb to challenge well-known historians has made no impact whatever. This present memoir, however egoistic, is a defiant gesture to show that I am still able to write and have not accepted defeat.

13

The Legacy

There are considerably better opportunities today for a young man or woman ambitious to pursue a career in military history than when I began in the late 1950s. There has been an enormous expansion in the number of universities, many with one or more specialist military historians. Consequently there are more openings to take undergraduate courses and go on to obtain an MA or PhD partly or even mainly related to the study of war.

Numerically there can be no doubt that the Department of War Studies at King's College, London is in a league of its own after an astonishing expansion since my retirement in 2001. The latest statistics are as follows: BA students 736, MA students 580, PhD candidates 200 and academic staff 70. However these figures must be treated with caution because 'War Studies' now covers a large majority of students focusing on contemporary international relations and security studies. A senior historian in the Department calculates that only about 20% of the BA course involves military history and, apart from a core course, only about 25% of the MA candidates study history. The ratio is better at PhD level with perhaps as many as a third pursuing topics with a strong historical basis. Only about 8 of the academic staff would describe themselves as military historians, which is only a small increase since my day.

In recent years, under the enthusiastic leadership of Gary Sheffield, Stephen Badsey and their colleagues, Wolverhampton has rapidly become a vibrant centre for the study of war and military history with its own Department. About 40 undergraduates per annum are admitted to study history, politics and war studies for a BA degree. About 60 to 70 part-time graduates study for an MA on line or take the options on the First World War (extremely popular) or the Second World War combined with the Holocaust. At present there are about 20 doctoral candidates, but this number is likely to increase considerably. Unlike some other universities where the study of war is regarded with suspicion, or worse, Wolverhampton receives strong support from the authorities.

Military history is also strongly represented in the Defence Studies Department at the Joint Services Command and Staff College, where my former doctoral student, Robert Foley, is now head of department. The College awards an MA degree in Defence Studies and International Relations.

Other prominent centres for the study of war and military history include University of Kent at Canterbury (with about six academic staff), Exeter, Leeds, and Queen Mary College, University of London. The University of Buckingham offers a Master's in Modern War Studies and Contemporary Military History based in central London. Clearly unless there is an established chair or lectureship (which are rare) numbers will fluctuate as senior scholars retire or move elsewhere. This may be true of Leeds and Exeter for example, but there is a good chance that where military history courses have become established in the syllabus younger members will be promoted or hired.

Of course it would be preposterous to claim that Sir Michael Howard and the Department he created at King's College, London have been wholly responsible for these developments, but it can be shown that several of our PhD 'ambassadors' have 'spread the gospel' in other British universities. To list only my own successful 'exports': John Gooch (Lancaster and Leeds), David French (U.C.L.), Ian Beckett (Luton and Kent at Canterbury), Gary Sheffield (Birmingham and Wolverhampton), Philip Towle (Cambridge), Jim Beach (Salford and Northampton), John Sweetman (Warwick), the late Alex Danchev (Keele and Nottingham), and Robert Foley (Liverpool and The Joint Services Command and Staff College). Brian Holden Reid also deserves inclusion having returned to King's College after nine years as the senior civilian academic at the Staff College, Camberley.

Professor Sir Hew Strachan has given me an informed personal impression of the universities with which he is familiar. Rather than try to summarise his report I quote it at length:

> St. Andrews has a greater critical mass in the study of war than Oxford does, and was ready to make two appointments as well as mine to demonstrate its commitment to the subject. We have set up an Institute for War and Strategy, and it is directly supported by five full-time members of

staff. At Oxford I was the only person in the Changing Character of War programme – at least by the end – who was in a permanent appointment. The University is ready to give both money and time to making the Institute prosper. This is all very different from my Oxford experience.

Let me answer your broader question in two ways. The first is the state of military history generally across the United Kingdom. Here I am upbeat: the effect of the introduction of market forces to almost all universities, except Oxford and Cambridge, has been to ensure that there is some military history now in most undergraduate offerings, precisely because it is popular. It is true that there are no more departments of military history, but in some senses that is no bad thing. It brings me back to the old refrain of the 1970s: military history is part of 'total' history, and I worry about military historians who have no idea of the broader political and economic context in which the events they are discussing are set. Premature and excessive specialisation seems to me to be narrowing the perspective of all historians, and military historians are no exception.

The second issue is that military history is making a comeback in the study of war and strategy more generally. I don't want to exaggerate this: political scientists and international relations experts have become woefully ignorant of history and are overly dependent on theory. But most of the centres for the study of war are inter-disciplinary – and that goes for the three I've been involved in at Glasgow, Oxford and St Andrews. What military historians have to do is to work out how best they can contribute to this discussion without compromising on their own standards, while engaging with other approaches. In some senses this is a throw-back to the use of military history by armies for professional reasons, but you and I know plenty of examples of the didactic use of military history in the past which have proved counterproductive. The essence seems to me to use military history to distinguish between change and continuity (rather than just stress the latter), and to generate an understanding of war.

You asked specifically about Edinburgh and Glasgow. Glasgow has made global security a theme across humanities and social sciences, and has therefore made a number of appointments to reflect that. So, for example, Peter Jackson, who now holds the Chair of Modern History, is described as a historian of global security. The Scottish Centre for

> War Studies, which I set up, is thriving, and has a full masters degree programme. Edinburgh's Centre for Second World War Studies, set up by Jeremy Crang and Paul Addison has turned into a Centre for War Studies, but it is still located in history.
>
> Finally, you may know that Oxford has made a second appointment in military history. This is what I had been pushing for all the time I was at Oxford, and it is ironical that it has happened since my departure. However, the fact that Peter Wilson (my successor), is an early modernist made it – in my view – inevitable. Fortunately David Parrott at New College took the same view. As an early modernist himself, he was ready to push his college into making an election in the history of modern war to replace Ruth Harris when she was elected to All Souls. The All Souls connection has worked in a reverse flow, as the person they have chosen is himself a former Prize Fellow named Alexander Morrison who works on Russia and central Asia. What remains to be seen is how far a core focus on the study of war will be really maintained.

It would be invidious to name names, but my colleagues and I have had some indirect influences, through former graduates in War Studies, at several public institutions concerned with our subject including: the House of Commons, the Imperial War Museum, the Army Records Society, the Air and Navy Historical Branches and the Royal United Services Institute.

More generally, the growing popularity of military history is to be seen in the publishing world and in the spread of special interest societies. As regards specialist publishers Pen and Sword is long-established and continues to promote the subject over a wide field. In recent years Helion Press has gained ground as a specialist military history publisher, while among general publishers Routledge has an impressive military history list.

To the list of long-established journals such as the *Mariner's Mirror*, *The Army Quarterly*, *The Journal of the Society for Army Historical Research* and *War in History* may now be added the *British Journal for Military History*. As regards societies, to older institutions such as the Army and Navy Records Societies may be added the British Commission for Military History (discussed earlier) and the Western Front Association, founded only in 1980 but already firmly established with branches throughout the British Isles and with affiliated branches in several overseas countries.

Why this recent surge in the popularity of military history and war studies? This is not the place for a detailed examination of this fascinating topic, but merely for a few suggestions which might be worth further study. First, war and conflict more generally are always with us as most exciting and controversial topics in the press and on television. Secondly, there are far more outlets now for reporters, commentators and security experts. None of the myriad of authors and speakers in these fields are King's College alumni to my knowledge, but clearly 'stars' like the late Richard Holmes, Frank Gardner and Max Hastings provide inspiration for a new generation of media pundits. Thirdly, with the armed services giving more emphasis to the importance of academic qualifications there is a strong incentive to take a degree in the highly relevant topics of military history and war studies. Fourthly, I will propose a paradox; namely that these subjects have acquired an enhanced attraction in our comparatively un-military society: National Service ended in the early 1960s; Britain has not been engaged in a major war for a generation; its Services' personnel have been drastically cut, and very few men in uniform are seen in public. Perhaps there is an element, and no more, of curiosity and nostalgia for a recent past of extreme danger and heroic national achievement?

As I have already suggested, the study of military history is now not only much more popular than it was when I began teaching at King's in 1966, it is also more *respectable*. This change was initially in large part due to the work and influence of Sir Michael Howard, who did much to replace the traditional 'drums and trumpets' approach with the broader concept of 'War and Society' with its cultural and political ramifications. Before him, Michael suggested, with only slight exaggeration, the numbers of scholars interested in war and conflict could be numbered on the fingers of one hand, whereas now it had become 'an overcrowded field'.

As regards the status of military history in British universities I would modify Michael's phrase to read 'a well-cultivated and productive field', but one which requires constant attention to ensure that the quantity and quality of its crops remain up to standard. There is not an urgent need for many more military history teachers and courses, but it is vital that the *respectability* of this academic discipline should be upheld, and the widespread placement of specialist scholars be maintained.

See also Appendix 2 for Professor Martin Alexander's review of 'The Military History/War Studies situation in the United Kingdom in March 2017'.

Afterword

Teaching at any level is very demanding on one's energy and nerves. I experienced the tension and tiredness in my brief periods in three very different schools in 1959–61 and developed a deep respect for the profession. It was my good fortune to spend most of my career teaching students who were keen to study my subject and had competed for a place. Even then I encountered individuals on the MA course who initially thought Clausewitz's *On War* was a load of (Prussian) rubbish and I was delighted if I could convert them in time for the exam.

If you do not enjoy teaching it can be very stressful indeed, as I noted in one or two sad cases at Borlase, but even if you did enjoy it the practice had to bring its own reward: there were no medals or trophies and very few honours. Looking back in retirement I asked myself, like most of the profession I imagine, if I had achieved anything. Where had all the decades gone? Just occasionally one would receive a cheering word of praise from a former student or, in later life, members of the audience bringing copies of one's book to sign. Recently I met an elderly couple who had driven up from the south coast to hear me lecture at Wolverhampton; a reassuring sign that one's efforts were appreciated. For another example, near the end of my time at King's I had a lively MA class who really enjoyed the discussion of one of their papers, and it was a 'red letter day' to find them still in debate in the stairwell when I left to go home.

At the most basic level I set high standards for spelling, punctuation and grammar on the assumption that most students would need to be literate when they later held responsible positions. Hence there could be no mixed metaphors, no 'comprised of' and no confusion between 'uninterested' and 'disinterested'. But when students began citing references from the press to back up their 'errors', for example on the new ubiquitous use of 'hopefully', I knew the game was lost. I also thought that the correct spelling of proper names was important and would jokingly remark that if, under exam pressure, students could spell Clausewitz, Bismarck and Rundstedt they deserved to pass.

Steering borderline candidates to success at BA, MA and PhD levels always brought pleasure. I recall an American student who aspired to go to West Point after King's but arrived with little notion of punctuation or paragraphs and was dismayed when I told him his first paper was a clear 'fail'. However he worked hard and improved to earn a 'distinction' mark in his final essay. He passed the MA exams and duly went to West Point. At the other extreme I taught another American with an engineering background whose first paper was so good I awarded it a straight 'alpha' – very unusual for me. That evening he rang me at home to apologise because he had had to rush the writing and felt it to be sub-standard! The essay duly appeared, essentially unchanged, in a learned journal. Of course this was an exceptional case: most of the time one was trying to help all students who were doing their best to attain, and even go beyond, what level they thought they could reach. But the most tantalising challenge, to which there was seldom proof of success, was so to stir the groups' enthusiasm and imagination that just one individual's mental outlook would be transformed for ever – as Charles Davenport had inspired me at Borlase c. 1950.

Readers who have stayed with this account so far will know that I have had a comparatively quiet, uneventful life. But there is one unusual aspect which perhaps does merit a few paragraphs: namely the living out of my entire adult life in one small village; namely Medmenham in the Thames Valley mid-way between Marlow and Henley. My mother was born in the village and lived there most of her life, while my father came from Frieth, only about three miles away. To my later regret I was born (in 1936) just on the Marlow side of the parish boundary, but apart from one year (1945–6) when my parents tried farming in Huntingdonshire, my home base has been in Medmenham ever since. It is a cliché, but still true, that this has given me 'deep roots' in the village's history, inhabitants and memorable events such as flooding. The debit side is that I have been very reluctant to move, and now hope I shall never need to. Over the decades I have developed an almost mystic empathy with this beautiful, secluded realm; running and swimming in my younger days and now enjoying the quiet and serenity of the woods, to which I have privileged access.

Since I first began singing in the choir in 1943 I have cherished a deep affection for the village church and churchyard. My parents were married here in 1924, and there is a whole row of graves for my mother's Sartin relatives. Moreover I remember a majority of the old villagers buried here since the Second World War. Sir Basil and Lady Liddell Hart are buried just beyond the west door, and some day I expect to lie close to them and to my parents.

Unlike my boyhood literary hero, William Hazlitt, I have had a tranquil career with few bitter quarrels. Hazlitt died aged 52 whereas I have survived beyond 80, but I am pleased to echo his final words: 'Well, I've had a happy life'.

Appendix I

The two reviews which alienated Lady Liddell Hart

Liddell Hart, a reassessment, by John Terraine

Liddell Hart: A Study of his Military Thought by Brian Bond. (Cassell. £7.95.)
Let me say at once that this is a very important and very valuable book. It must have been hell to write. The late Sir Basil Liddell Hart was unquestionably the most prolific and persuasive military commentator of this century, surpassing in influence his friend and mentor, Maj-Gen. J. F. C. Fuller.

Brian Bond also became his friend, and owes him an acknowledged debt of gratitude for much kindness and support, especially in the difficult early stages of making his own career as a military historian. That kindness and helpfulness to selected people was one of the most agreeable qualities of Liddell Hart. It had, however, a reverse side: a vindictive malice with which he pursued other selected targets, especially when his deep vanity was touched.

As one who incurred this malice I merely record that he *could* be kind, and set it to his credit. What must have made "Liddell Hart: a Study of His Military Thought" so difficult for Mr Bond is the recollection of kindness on the one hand and a growing sense of his friend's fallibility on the other.

The fallibility is not entirely news; I am not alone in being endlessly surprised at the respect – indeed, adulation – which continues to be heaped on Liddell Hart. And here we see the truth set out, clearly if reluctantly, by one who would obviously have preferred to say other things.

It is not, of course, that one disagrees with everything that Liddell Hart said; he fought on too many fronts for total disagreement. What he says, for example, about Roosevelt's policy of "Unconditional Surrender" is exactly what

Fuller says, and I agree with both. I agree about the Hiroshima bomb. I agree about war guilt trials and the treatment of captured enemy generals.

On all those issues, and on many others, Liddell Hart was right. What he was wrong about, unfortunately, was the central military facts of this century up to 1945. His whole reputation as a military writer was, in fact, founded upon a set of almost ridiculous misapprehensions.

Liddell Hart advertised himself—he was very good at that—and was, indeed is, widely accepted as a cool scientific thinker about war. At bottom he was nothing of the kind. He was a man in a permanent state of shock deriving from his brief but traumatic experience on the Western Front in the first world war. His most famous theories stem not from science but from shock.

Thus "The British Way in Warfare", (1932), ostensibly a plea for a return to "traditional," "maritime" strategy as opposed to continental commitment, is simply a recoil from the "bloodbaths" of the Western Front. The cool truth (which Mr Bond perceives and states) is that the "British way" was generally disastrous, and could never work against a major enemy unless we could find someone else willing to do all the dying. Not easy.

It is the same with the famous theory of the "Indirect Approach." Liddell Hart always made this sound very "scientific" and historical. The essence of it is to be found in his biography of General Sherman (1929) which, as Mr Bond says, "occupies a unique place in his intellectual development."

What he never saw, never *was able* to see was that Sherman's famous manoeuvre 'against the Confederate rear, was only made possible by the battles of attrition which Grant was conducting in Virginia. Fuller saw that, and in the end gave "Indirect Approach" its right name: "the strategy of Evasion." But Fuller was a historian.

Liddell Hart on total war is a similar case; he was "against" total war. He might just as well have been against Thursday, or technology, or the French Revolution. Fuller saw, but Liddell Hart never did, that total war is the natural method of industrialised mass societies fighting for survival, and that this is particularly so in democracies.

The totality was, in fact, an attribute of the democracy. It was pointless to be "against" it: the thing for a sharp, nimble brain like Liddell Hart's to be considering was how to deal with the dreadful thing. But no. Instead he began that process which Mr Bond calls "forcing history to yield the appropriate lessons." In other words, faking.

All this is sad, but in no way detracts from Brian Bond's admirable book. He writes with courage and wisdom, and providing that you can stand some of the nonsense he has to examine he is a pleasure to read.

From: *The Daily Telegraph*, 25 August 1977

Mind Behind The Front
The Marquess of Anglesey

Liddell Hart: A Study of His Military Thought by Brian Bond, Cassell, 280pp, £7.95.

Who wrote in 1916 that Haig was "the greatest general Britain had ever owned"? None other than the most famous military critic of the 20th century, who spent much of the next 53 years decrying and defaming British generalship in the First World War.

As Hore-Belisha's *éminence grise* in 1937–38, Captain Basil Liddell Hart also preached that the defensive was so superior that it was virtually unthinkable that an aggressor could ever again execute a successful offensive. For that monumental misjudgment he suffered a well merited eclipse during the Second World War.

Brian Bond, Lecturer in War Studies at King's College, London, was friend, neighbour and research assistant to the subject of this discerning, well-written book. In it he makes a gallant attempt to explain how a man who could be so chronically wrong came to be acknowledged by successful German, Israeli and even British generals as their guru, and to be revered by countless students of war.

There is no photograph of "the Captain who taught Generals" in Liddell Hart: A Study of his Military Thought. This omission is in line with Lady Liddell Hart's decision that biographical information should be confined to what was necessary for an appreciation of her husband's ideas.

Beside, therefore, roaming references to a Wesleyan minister father, a spoiling mother, two wives and his 6ft. 4in. height (so different from the tiny stature of General Fuller, his mentor and fellow military theorist), the reader must expect few personal details. Mr. Bond does tell us, though, that Liddell Hart was peculiarly vulnerable to flattery.

His professional, purely military reputation began with his revolutionary ideas on infantry tactics during and after the First World War. It was increased by his theories of the "expanding torrent" and the strategy of "indirect approach." It was consolidated by his belief in out-and-out mechanisation.

Where Fuller proclaimed the all-tank army, Liddell Hart, at any rate at first, relied on an infantry element. Later, he, even more than Fuller, argued for fully mechanised infantry and supply columns. Without the mobility and speed these would confer, "an army," he wrote in 1927, "is but a corpse—awaiting burial in a trench."

His personal experience of trench warfare was slight, but his studies of the Western Front campaigns, their horrors and above all their monstrous casualties went deep. So did his extreme aversion to violence. All this implanted in his brilliant, if rather innocent, mind an ever-increasing resolve that Britain should never again become entrapped in a Continental war.

It was this obsession, combined with an inordinate political naivety, that led him, against increasing evidence to the contrary, to believe that Hitler was a rational statesman no different from, say, Louis XIV or Napoleon, and to press through most of the war for a negotiated peace He went so far, for example, as to rebuke Bertrand Russell "for abandoning pacifism and applauding the war"!

In short, as a tactical theorist he was admirable. So much so that Mr. Bond can claim, perhaps without exaggeration, that Liddell Hart's supreme achievement may have been "to transform the nature of military thought itself." But as soon as he left his specialist, restricted field he was all at sea, descending almost to silliness. Yet even in the wider spheres into which he ventured, he often played the role of beneficial gadfly.

He was almost frenetically industrious: his output of polemical articles, chiefly as military correspondent of *The Daily Telegraph* and later of the *Times*, as a writer of letters to influential people and as a serious historian, was enormous. It was his habit to keep every letter he received, every note he ever made. Mr. Bond's labour of love must have been laborious indeed. The result fully justifies his exertions.

From: *The Sunday Telegraph*, 28 August 1977

Appendix II

Military History and War Studies in the UK – A review in September 2017 by Martin Alexander – Professor Emeritus, Aberystwyth University

---

Every bookshop demonstrates the flourishing of work in military history and the study of war. There, as the website of the online *BJMH (British Journal for Military History)*, launched in 2015, justifiably states: '"Military History" shelves often take up as much space as does mere "History". Even those whose primary interest is not military history as such now realise that a knowledge of the subject is necessary if they are to understand the past, to say nothing of the present. 'Military history is now too important to be left to the military historians.' But before commenting further on this sense of a subject's current confident position – and the ups and downs of teaching, writing and publishing about war's past and present – some caveats.

First: a 'state of the field' survey can offer only a health-check akin to a motor car's annual MoT test – that is, a snapshot of what is what, who is where, and the working condition of the sub-discipline. Such a snapshot can only picture a moment, one that may prove fleeting. So this short postscript essay to the memoirs of Brian Bond (who gave highly valued help in my career development) makes no claim to be comprehensive, nor does it warrant that what is said in good faith now will long remain a reliable guide.

Second: the remarks that follow are neither more nor less than personal. They are prompted by my engagement since the later 1970s with military historians and the overlapping scholarly communities in and outside the UK universities – communities that study and reflect seriously on war and the connected sub-specialisations of defence policy, intelligence and espionage studies, military sociology, and strategic theory.

Right away, it bears saying that the study of military history and kindred sub-disciplines is by and large in fine fettle. The *BJMH* is correct: the outpouring of publications on war and its history is voluminous, wide-ranging, more diverse than was the case a hundred, fifty or even thirty years ago. War's study by historians has experienced its own version of a 'cultural turn' – if probably never going full-on Postmodemist – as Jeremy Black reflected in his book *Rethinking Military History* (Routledge: 2004). The flow of well-researched and ever more imaginatively framed books since the mid-1990s, and the existence of a strong body of scholarly periodicals such as *War in History* (launched 1994), together with the longer-lived and US-based *Journal of Military History,* attest to the vigorous health and quantity of military-historical studies.

There is an encouraging diversification in methodologies, our subject(s) being approached via a wide lens. There is military history from 'on high' such as Gary Sheffield's *The Chief: Douglas Haig and the British Army* (Aurum: 2011) and – much diversified since the pioneering book of Eric Hobsbawm, *Bandits* (Weidenfeld & Nicolson, 1969) – 'from below' such as Catherine Merridale's *Ivan's War: Life and Death in the Red Army, 1939–45* (Faber: 2005). Work coming at war 'from the side', one might say, has also flourished recently by bringing out the roles of women, children, civilians, military medicine, animals and the environment, *vide* the innovative work of Chris Pearson of Liverpool University on militarized landscapes and war's environmental history *(Mobilising Nature :* Manchester UP: 2012), Nicole Dombrowski-Risser's *France under Fire* (Cambridge UP: 2012) on civilian flight and family survival in 1939–45 France, or Stefan Goebel and Derek Keene on urban agglomerations as combat zones *(Cities into Battlefields:* Ashgate 2011). Such breadth attests to the exciting expansion of the topics around war – and approaches to war – that are judged right, fit and fascinating in the C21st.

Perhaps there is, as a consequence, something of a danger that a 'fog of war studies' has also ensued from the opening wide of the optics through which armed conflict is conceptualized, framed and researched. Has this caused some opacity or fuzziness around what military history and war studies now means, or has as its 'core business'? Not long after Jeremy Black's volume appeared a point had evidently been reached where Stephen Morillo and Michael F. Pavkovic brought out *What is Military History ?* (Polity: 2006). It would be a challenging question indeed to ask for a concise definition of a subject that has now evolved so far from chronicling past clashes between (dead) White men or between (dead) White men and (many more) dead non-White men – along with butchery of unnumbered non-White women and children. Perspectives have shifted; terms once employed with little thought are now sharply contested. A blog about the Little Big Horn fight in Montana with Custer's 7th Cavalry in 1876 asked pertinently why actions that killed quantities of White (or 'European') soldiers are called 'massacres' (e.g. the 1860 Fetterman 'massacre' of 81 US cavalry troopers) whereas, bizarrely, those inflicting one-sided slaughter on indigenous populations, as at Sand Creek in 1864 or the Washita in 1868, are invariably called 'battles'?

In the 1970s it was a 'war and society' approach that flourished. This was pioneered in Britain through Open University courses from 1969 and framed one of the books by Brian Bond, his *War and Society in Europe 1870–1970* (Fontana: 1983). Yet operational and combat history, frowned upon in academe for many years, roared back strongly from the late 1980s onwards. Sophisticated, seriously-researched expressions of it seen lately include William Philpott's *Attrition: Fighting the First World War* (Little Brown: 2014) and John Buckley's *Monty's Men. The British Army and the Liberation of Europe* (Yale UP: 2014). These stand well alongside the kinds of cultural and gender perspectives exemplified by work like Joanna Bourke's *An Intimate History of Killing: Face-to-Face Killing in Twentieth Century Warfare* (Granta: 1999) on the attraction to some men of lethal violence, as licensed and encouraged in the mayhem of war.

For today's surely broad definitions, military history/war studies has travelled far beyond the points that were at its core when 'bugles and trumpets' was the dominant written genre, the focus on uniforms, medals, tactics and battles devoid of political, economic, socio-cultural or gendered contexts. It seems therefore bizarre that not much over 20 years ago Lawrence H. Keeley could assert in a chapter entitled 'The Roots of the Pacified Past', in his book *War Before Civilization* (Oxford UP: 1996), that academic interest in military history had become so anaemic as to be 'relegated to a few professors at provincial institutions and the military academies, to nonacademics, and to amateurs' – a picture of military history studies unrecognizable to Andrew Linklater, Woodrow Wilson Chair of International Relations at Aberystwyth, who has called this a simply 'extraordinary claim'.

Nor is intelligence, espionage and covert operations still a 'missing dimension' in military history. Far from it. Today the Cinderella subject within-the-subject is surely the 'Q' branch of armies, navies and air forces – the quartermasters and the organising of logistics, supply, transport, communications, medical and veterinary services. Despite seminal books by, among others, Martin van Creveld (*Supplying War:* Cambridge UP, 1977) and John Lynn (*Feeding Mars:* Westview Press, 1994) it remains frustratingly hard to promote publications about military supply and transport. Yet a range of curiously unfashionable tail and rear-echelon military services was – and is – essential to sustain any military campaign. It was long ago averred that 'amateurs talk tactics, professionals talk logistics'. All the same, this topic remains a kind of backwater with limited appeal both to publishers and postgraduate students seeking topics for university theses.

The cultural study of war, along with echoes of war in prose, poetry, comic books, art, architecture, music etc. is, however, most certainly thriving. One indication is the prominence of the 'school' around Jay Winter (though this may start to show some decline, since Professor Winter retired from Yale in December 2014). In France, meanwhile, many scholars are associated with the *Historial de la Grande Guerre* at Péronne and the books of some of them, including Annette Becker and Stephane Audoin-Rouzeau, have appeared in English editions whilst in Britain there is an International Society for First World War Studies founded by Jenny Macleod and Pierre Purseigle.

Much of war's broad and rich historical treatment today is attributable to the fine work of organisations such as the British Commission for Military History (BCMH), Society for Army Historical Research, and the Western Front Association (WFA). These have enjoyed strong leadership e.g. the BCMH under Brian Bond, then Richard Holmes and Mungo Melvin; the Army Records Society under John Gooch and now Matthew Hughes; the WFA under the eminent and congenial Peter Simkins MBE (President since 2011), his immediate predecessor Correlli 'Bill' Barnett CBE, and further back the pioneering work of John Terraine, a crucially influential early revisionist about the 1914–18 British army.

Such associational bodies act as umbrellas. They also serve as conduits. In the latter function they 'reach out' both effectively and inclusively. They and their committees have shown skill in linking and expanding varied military history communities. They have, thank goodness, acted as lumpers not splitters. It is evident that we are not too far off eliminating the unhelpful old apartheids of professionals-vs.-amateur and university academics-vs.-independents. Those separations were pernicious and damaging. They bred scholarly snobbery;

they led to camps, cliques and compartmentalisation. There is far less of that today, and far more healthy respect and two-way tolerance. The WFA has over 6,000 members and 63 branches in the UK, Ireland, the Commonwealth and North America at present (including affiliated bodies). It does great work as a link between academics and the informed general public. The addition of Sir Hew Strachan as Patron of the WFA adds to its scholarly reputation. This widening scholarly influence can also be detected in the major growth in well-run battlefield tours and battlefield archaeology, with professionalized accreditation owing much to the Guild of Battlefield Guides and being exemplified by respected figures like Jack Sheldon and Steve Roberts.

Nonetheless, it may be prudent to remember the concern of Lawrence H. Keeley in 1996 that 'by the middle of the twentieth century, history professors at prestigious universities were concerned almost exclusively with social and economic matters.' There was some basis for this downbeat analysis in regard to North American academe, although an upswing was noticeable from the later 1980s when Paul M. Kennedy, crossing the Atlantic from the University of East Anglia, developed a major military and strategic history doctoral and postdoctoral programme at Yale (generously funded by the John M. Olin Foundation and other grant-givers), whilst Sir Michael Howard retired from the Regius Chair of Modern History at Oxford in 1989 to move to Yale to inaugurate the Robert M. Lovett Chair of Military and Naval History.

In British universities, too, the study of warfare, strategy and military history assumed greater prominence and prestige in the early 1990s with leadership positions for Brian Bond, Professor of Military History at KCL, Colin S. Gray, Professor of Strategic Studies at the University of Hull from 1992 (and from 1999 at the University of Reading) and John Gooch, who from 1992 was Professor of International History at the University of Leeds where Edward Spiers held the Chair of Strategic Studies.

Academic fashions ebb and flow; the wheels of human affairs turn (and turn again). From the standpoint of 2017, perhaps military history and war studies enjoyed a short-lived 'golden age' about 15–20 years ago. A vigorous expansion certainly occurred of military history and war studies degree schemes with teaching staff appointed in great numbers. This was the case from Glasgow and Edinburgh via Salford, Leeds and Hull to Aberystwyth, Birmingham, then Wolverhampton, and Reading and Kent. War and intelligence studies also appeared on the curriculum in Greater London e.g. at Brunel University, beyond the ever-popular and respected Department of War Studies at King's College. In this era this clutch of universities constructed – in the academic *lingua franca* of the time – a 'critical mass' of staff and research postgraduates. They were fed from below by a healthy crop of BA, BSc(Econ) and taught Master's students working on military history and congruent sub-fields.

Some of these clusters remain thriving – or at least holding their own – in 2017. One is Brunel, which has Matthew Hughes, Philip Davies and Kristof Gustafson. Another is the University of Exeter. There a Centre for the Study of War and Society was established under the leadership of Martin Thomas in 2005. The University of Warwick has also enjoyed dynamic expansion with Richard Aldrich as Professor of Intelligence Studies (having in 1989–92 set up Salford University's MA in Intelligence and International Relations and then a Chair-holder for many years at Nottingham University). The University of Kent (with campuses now at Chatham and Canterbury), also has great strength on its staff including Gaynor Johnson (ex-Salford), Mark Connelly and Tim Bowman.

John Bourne, whilst at the University of Birmingham from the 1980s to early 2000s had a crucial and inspirational role in creating a centre of excellence for First World War Studies there. His MA course in First World War Studies has provided the template for the Wolverhampton course. Several of John Bourne's mature MA students – such as Trevor Harvey and Peter Hodgkinson – have gone on to PhDs and become heavyweight scholars in their own right. Gary Sheffield maintained this legacy at Birmingham (as has Jonathan Boff) before he transferred to Wolverhampton. Professor Sheffield's influence in picking up the baton from John Terraine to re-assess more favourably both Douglas Haig and the 1914–18 British Army – particularly its command style and combat achievements – has been hugely important in off-setting an older dominant narrative of British soldiers and generals resembling 'lions led by donkeys'.

Wolverhampton University's expansion of staff, students and short courses in war studies and military history may currently give it a fair claim to be second in the UK only to KCL War Studies and its associated Department of Defence Studies at the Shrivenham-Watchfield staff college. John Buckley at Wolverhampton, reinforced by Stephen Badsey, Spencer Jones and others, have built an impressive cluster and now have John Bourne there as Honorary Professor of First World War Studies, with Peter Simkins the Honorary Professor of Western Front Studies. The big beneficiary of Birmingham's retreat from very much study of warfare is its West Midlands rival.

True, as well, is that academic 'lone rangers' in war studies can still be found: individual tutor-scholars scattered about, teaching a module here and a module there. Yet how many UK universities have absolutely no staff or courses that do not in some sense, from some disciplinary perspective, touch on war in the past or present? At Edinburgh there is still the Centre for the Study of Two World Wars (originally the Centre for the Study of the Second World War), whilst up the coast at St Andrews there is Sir Hew Strachan, the distinguished successor at several removes from Sir Michael Howard in the Chichele Chair of the History of War at Oxford.

The story of Birmingham University's Chair in War Studies, briefly existing after 2006, was not the happiest; but the institution still has a Royal Aeronautical Society sponsored Senior Fellow in Airpower Studies held by Air Cdre (Retd) Dr Peter Gray, as well as lecturers whose work lies firmly within military history such as Jonathan Boff.

At Aberystwyth the degree schemes and staffing in intelligence – military history – strategic studies boomed in the years 1996 to about 2012, but then underwent severe cuts. Experienced staff left (Martin Alexander and Len Scott retiring in 2014); others went to posts elsewhere without successors coming in at a comparable seniority e.g. Peter Jackson to a Chair at Glasgow in 2013, Huw Bennett and Madeline Carr to Cardiff in 2015, Alastair Finlan to the Royal Swedish Defence Academy in 2016.

Mostly, however, I am an optimist about the state of the discipline. I feel this optimism is warranted paradoxically because of the very widespread pessimism about the state of the world. Students now at university were children as the Iraq and Afghan conflicts after 9/11 unfolded across their television screens, as the Arab Spring exploded onto their iPhones in 2011–13, and as urban war among the ruins of Aleppo and Mosul along with North Korea's repeated nuclear weapon tests saturate media outputs now. Today's young know that their time is truly an 'age of wars'. They assuredly want to study military affairs, violent conflicts, terrorism and counter-insurgency in all the field's multiple, complex manifestations. They crave better comprehension via imaginative but serious teaching, well-researched but accessible books, and robust but clear methodologies.

About 120 people, all paying their own travel and day-school costs, attended the WFA's annual President's Conference in Edgbaston in June 2016. That month, also, some two hundred people packed into Wolverhampton University for Gary Sheffield's centenary lecture on the Battle of the Somme.

At Aberystwyth, 57 percent of the undergraduates in session 2015–16 in the Department of International Politics opted for one or more modules on topics in military and international history, strategy, intelligence/espionage – whereas not 20 percent of the staff specialized in those sub-fields. Over 100 students at Aberystwyth – standing room only – filled a hall in February 2017 to hear Owen Bennett-Jones of the BBC World Service and *London Review of Books* lecture about operations and intelligence against Islamic State and Al-Qaeda.

Students, more so than many university staff, are keenly interested in getting to grips with studying and better understanding war, strategy, defence policy and intelligence (fuelled by the Wikileaks scandals?). It is because they 'get' the old dictum of Lenin and the Bolsheviks, as true in 2017 as it was in 1917: 'You may not be interested in war, but war will be interested in you'.

Moreover various 'A' Level units are thriving in the subject area: OCR's 'The Changing Nature of Warfare 1792–1945' and Edexcel's similar 'The changing nature of warfare, 1859–1991: perception and reality'. There is also Edexcel's 'The British experience of warfare, c.1790–1918' and OCR's 'A' Level unit on 'The Middle East 1908–2011: Ottomans to Arab Spring' and its two units on the Cold War: 'Asia 1945–1993' and 'Europe 1941–1995'. Within what one might call the general history units – i.e. not listed as specifically warfare related – campaigns and battles crop up throughout. This is most evident in detail in the unit dealing with 'The USA in the 19th Century: Westward expansion and Civil War 1803–c.1890', where many American Civil War campaigns and battles are specified for Sixth Form study.

This assessment only dips a toe into what might be a much more detailed analysis of the position of Military History at 'A' Level. Interestingly the graphics on the cover of the new OCR 'A' Level Specification flag up aspects to do with studying warfare. That there are these units currently at 'A' Level is encouraging for the future of the specialisation. That they have survived for so long, since approximately 1999/2000, suggests a buoyant clientele in British schools and Sixth Form colleges that will needs to be catered for in the universities. And these studies should flourish because war is a central part of the human condition, set to remain so whether the academy always takes it with due seriousness or not.